LOOK BACK *For What?*

"SOMETIMES THE ONLY WAY
FORWARD IS TO LOOK BACK"

TELESA SMITH WRIGHT

WWW.LOOKBACKFORWHAT.COM

Foreword

As I sit down to write this foreword,

I am reminded of a journey—one filled with pain, doubt, faith, and triumph. This is not just my story; it's the story of so many who have felt broken, unworthy, and weighed down by the traumas of their past. It's for the woman who feels like her circumstances define her.

It's for the person who feels trapped by the voices of others, those voices that tell you who you are, what you will become, and how far you will go. This book is for you. And it's also for me, because writing it was part of my healing too.

I never imagined that my life, full of challenges and heartbreak, would one day be shared in these pages. For years, I carried the weight of rejection, the sting of abandonment, and the constant need to prove myself. I believed that if I worked hard enough, if I succeeded enough, I could silence the doubts that lived in the corners of my mind. But as I have come to learn, healing doesn't come from external achievements. Healing comes from within—from learning to forgive yourself, to forgive others, and to trust God to order your steps.

In these pages, you will read true stories of trauma, pain, and mistakes—but you will also read about resilience, faith, and redemption. You will see how God took my broken pieces and shaped them into something beautiful. You will walk with me through my fears, my moments of uncertainty, and my quiet prayers for more. And you will witness the incredible power of walking in faith, even when the path seems unclear.

"Look Back for What" is more than just a memoir. It's a testament to what happens when you choose faith over fear, forgiveness over bitterness, and love over resentment. It's about the moments when I realized that the voices of doubt, shame, and guilt were not the ones I needed to listen to. Instead, I began to listen to the voice of God—the voice that spoke of purpose, healing, and hope. And when I did, everything changed.

This book is a reflection of my heart. It's for anyone who has ever felt stuck, who has been told they wouldn't make it, who has battled with their past. It's for those who need a reminder that their story isn't over yet—that God can take whatever you've been through and use it for something greater than you could ever imagine.

As you read, my hope is that you see yourself in these pages. I hope that you are inspired to look within, to confront the things that have held you back, and to step into the life you were meant to live. We all have wounds, but those wounds can become the very source of our strength if we allow them to.

This is not a story of perfection—it's a story of progress. It's not about having it all figured out—it's about trusting the process. My prayer is that "Look Back for What" speaks to your heart and encourages you to keep moving forward, no matter what you've faced.

Thank you for joining me on this journey. May you find healing, hope, and the courage to live your life in the fullness of who you are meant to be.

With love and gratitude,

Telesa Smith Wright

Dedication

To My Husband, Benjamin:

You are the absolute best. You've seen me through so many phases of my life, and the last eighteen years with you have been precious. Thank you for showing me what agape love looks and feels like. You are my headache and my hero. I love who you are and appreciate all you do. There's no one else I'd rather do life with.

To My Children: Ambrisha, Jeremy, Trey, Jimee, Isaiah, and Jeremiah:

You each have taught me so much and continue to teach me every day. You have inspired me, challenged me, and helped me become the best version of myself. Thank you for your patience and your grace. My love for you all has revealed both the best and the worst in me, and I am better because of you.

To My Grandchildren; Jakobe, Jamir, and Zion:

Becoming "Yaya" has been one of my greatest joys. I promise to give you the best version of myself, to love you with abandon, to correct you in love, and to guide you with wisdom. You are a huge part of my inspiration, and I promise to leave a legacy you will be proud of.

To My Mom, Fannie:

We've come a long way together. You were not perfect, and I wasn't always the easiest child, but here we stand, having overcome so much. You may not have had resources, education, or support, but you had dreams, and you gave those dreams to me. Thank you for never shooting down my astronomical goals. I love you so much. Sometimes, it's not about what you're doing—it's about who you're raising.

To My Found Family and Friends:

My friends are like sisters, and I am grateful for every one of you. To the friend who's been there the entire ride: you make me laugh when I want to cry, you remind me who I am when I forget, and you bring perspective when I lose sight. Thank you for loving me and my family.

To My Readers and Supporters:

Thank you for joining me on this journey. I hope that through these pages, you find something that resonates with you. I want you to know that it is possible to change the course of your life. It starts with a decision and the courage to follow through.

Contents

Introduction

We've all heard the phrase, "Don't look back—you're not going that way." While there's truth to that idea, sometimes, to truly move forward, we must look back.

We need to revisit the places and moments where we've felt stuck, the stories we've told ourselves, and the traumas we've tried to forget. It's not about living in the past, but about uncovering the roots of the obstacles that keep us from living fully in the present. This book, Look Back For What, is about that process—about why sometimes looking back is essential for moving forward.

I've learned from personal experience that unresolved pain, buried traumas, and the stories we carry from our past can form invisible barriers to growth. You might have a vision of the life you want to live, a dream you want to pursue, or a desire for healing, but it feels as though something is always holding you back. You take two steps forward, only to find yourself back where you started. Why is that? It's because the things we haven't dealt with—the experiences we've left unprocessed—don't simply disappear. They stay with us, influencing our decisions, shaping our relationships, and keeping us from finding peace.

Today, I am a mother of six, a yaya of three, and the wife of an incredible man for eighteen years. I am an elevation coach, an entrepreneur, and a woman living the life I envisioned for myself—one filled with grace and growth, and the life God gifted me when I began to see myself clearly.

What I want more than anything is to share my journey, my stories, with others. I am not where I am today because of luck. I am here because God honored my request, and because I made decisions that reflected the life I wanted. I hope, in sharing my experiences, that you find something that causes a shift in your life.

This book is filled with real-life events of both trauma and victory. It's my sincere prayer that in reading these pages, you can identify your own traumas, understand the impact they've had on your life, and find a path to healing. It may hurt to look back, but when we do so with the right intention, we can begin to heal and move forward.

I was almost certain that I had healed but

In my early forties, I realized that I was still carrying the weight of trauma—still, in many ways, a walking ball of pain. Many of my responses, my actions, my tendencies were all rooted in past wounds. From withdrawing to lashing out, from my inability to say no to my obsession with perfection—it was all trauma-driven.

Again, the stories in this book are real, and they include my relationship with my mother. Today, my mom and I have a beautiful relationship. We worked through some of our issues, she allowed me to express my pain, and she stood by me through the process of healing. I share my stories not to demonize her, but to show that growth and healing are possible, even after years of hurt.

My mom wanted to understand me, to help me, to love me through it all. I hope that by reading this, you will be able to understand when she appears as the "villain" in my story.

She didn't always get it right, but she tried—and for that, I love her deeply.

My journey is one of healing, and I hope that it inspires you to find your own path to wholeness and joy.

In this book, we'll explore what it means to look back with purpose. We'll examine why some of the most challenging aspects of our past continue to show up in our present, and more importantly, how we can finally release them. This is a journey of healing, growth, and discovery, one that requires honesty and courage. Together, we'll learn how to embrace our stories, not to be trapped by them, but to be empowered by what they can teach us.

Throughout the pages ahead, you'll find reflections on healing from trauma, growing through hardship, and finding your purpose in the midst of it all. I'll share personal stories of the times I felt most stuck, when moving forward seemed impossible, and how looking back was the very thing that set me free. You'll also find practical insights and tools to help you reflect on your own journey—because the most important person you'll meet in this book is yourself.

Healing is not a straight path. Growth is not always linear. But what I've come to realize is that the detours, setbacks, and pauses along the way are all part of the process. They bring clarity, strength, and sometimes, the very breakthroughs we need to step into the life we're meant to live. It's time to stop running from the past and start using it as a tool for transformation.

So, why look back? Because sometimes, the keys to unlocking your future are hidden in the places you've been avoiding. Look Back For What is about confronting those places, and in doing so, finding the freedom to heal, grow, and truly live. This is your invitation to begin that journey. Let's start by looking back—so that together, we can finally move forward.

Chapter 1

Self-Reflection

I was desperate. My life was unraveling, and I felt broken beyond repair—damaged by dreams that never came true. I had no hope, no peace, no joy. The love I longed for seemed out of reach, and I had yet to learn how to truly love myself.

Generations of pain hung over my life like a dark cloud that wouldn't lift. Generational curses robbed me of innocence, binding me in cycles of abuse and addiction. I carried severe abandonment issues and unhealed childhood trauma, often letting them drive my choices and behavior.

I became whatever I needed to be to survive each moment, conforming to the situation. Poor decisions piled up until I no longer recognized the person staring back at me in the mirror. All I could see was shame, disgrace, and defeat, born from unwanted touches, misguided affection, and failures. No matter how many baths I took, the stench of shame lingered.

I hated the person I had become. I hated the disappointments I brought upon my mother and the recklessness I chose repeatedly. I had lost the core of who I was and became skilled at pretending I belonged in places I never should have been. Each mistake made it easier to justify the next.

I was raised with high values, but looking at myself then, it felt as if I had not been raised at all. I covered my pain with false confidence, sarcasm, and a superficial love for myself. On the outside, I looked as though I had it together; on the inside, I was dying a slow, painful death.

No one seemed to discern that the "diva" they saw—the woman with polished appearances and multiple boyfriends—was a mask. Beneath it was a broken little girl crying out for help. I wished someone could see beyond the facade, could see the pain behind my smile. My childhood had been taken from me, and I was never given a real chance. I was told I was an abomination to God, and without a loving earthly father, I felt fatherless in every sense.

I was lost. I had been taught religion, but not spirituality. Beaten down by those who should have protected me, I faced rejection and chaos from birth—born to a fourteen-year-old mother and a married twenty-eight-year-old father. It set the stage for a long road filled with pain.

I had reached the end of myself. Life didn't seem worth living, and I saw no way out of the pain except through death. But I had children who depended on me. Even though I wondered if they'd be better off without me, I knew my pain clouded my judgment. I remembered my mother's suicide attempt and the wound it left in me. I knew I couldn't leave my children with that same pain, but I still didn't know how to keep going.

One night, as tears ran down my face, I screamed for help. I cried out to God, "Please send help." Suddenly, something changed. The atmosphere shifted, and I felt an unexplained presence—a light, a gentle hug. It gave me a glimpse of hope. I believed it was God coming for me.

I was still unsure about life; suicide was still on the table. But that night, I found a second wind—enough strength to get to the next moment. Looking back now, I know my steps were being guided. A few days later, I found myself in line to pay a bill. I thought it would be terrible to leave my mother with my children and my debt—sarcasm that was just enough to keep me moving forward.

While in line, someone called my name. It was one of the pastors from a family I served as a waitress. They were always kind, considerate, and generous—different from others. He greeted me warmly, saying, "Hey, sister!" Then, to my surprise, he asked, "Why don't you join us for church this Sunday?" I replied "Yes" before I even thought about it. I wasn't sure I'd still be alive by Sunday, but I knew I had to keep my word.

That Sunday, I found myself in the small church parking lot. I sat in my car for a while, unsure of why I was there. Someone from the church walked out and waved at me— they saw me. I couldn't leave now.

I went inside and cried through the whole service. I couldn't tell you the message that day, but I remember standing up to leave and somehow ending up at the altar. The pastor asked what was stopping me from surrendering my life to God, and I said my life was a mess. He looked at me and said, "A well man doesn't need a doctor. You don't need to figure it all out before coming to God. Come to Him, and He will help you figure it out."

I prayed, "If you're real, God, you know what a mess I am. If you want this mess, you can have it." I believe God embraced me in that moment. My life wasn't suddenly easy, but I had a reason to keep going. With God, prayer, and intentional action, my life began to change.

I realized I could make excuses for where I was, or I could make adjustments to get where I wanted to be. I could let others write my story, or I could take the pen and be the author of my own journey. I didn't have to be what others expected me to be; I could set my own expectations.

I decided I could be both things at once:

- ↬ I could be a human mistake AND still make an impact.
- ↬ I could be a statistic AND a success story.
- ↬ I could be a screw-up AND change my course.
- ↬ I could be a teen mom AND create a life of stability for my children.
- ↬ I could come from a single-parent household AND learn to nurture a marriage.
- ↬ -I could come from poverty AND create wealth.

I had been raised one way, but I could raise myself anew. This was the beginning of my intentional growth process.

Quote:

"I could make excuses for where I was, or I could make adjustments to get where I wanted to be. I didn't have to be what others expected me to be; I could set my own expectations."

Chapter 2

Quieting the voices

I spent most of my life trying to drown out the voices. They were always there—reminding me of everything I wasn't and would never be. They echoed the judgments others made about me until those words became my own.

The Voices of Circumstance

The voices started early. I was born into circumstances that led others to draw conclusions about who I was and who I would become. My mother was fourteen when she had me, and my father, already married, was 28. I was "the other child," born of an affair in a deeply religious community—a source of shame and condemnation from the beginning.

I grew up hearing whispers about my birth, about my mother, about how I was destined to repeat her mistakes. The voices told me I would turn out just like her, that I was destined for failure. No matter how much I tried to ignore them, they seeped in and shaped my self-image and future.

The voices reminded me that I was an outsider, a mistake. They listed my failures, whispered that my worth was conditional, that I had to prove myself—and even then, it might not be enough.

Driven by Naysayers

For much of my life, I was driven by those voices. I was determined to prove them wrong—to show that I wasn't a mistake, that I could rise above my circumstances. I told myself I'd be different, that I wouldn't repeat my mother's mistakes, that I would be someone worth respecting.

Initially, being driven by the naysayers gave me fire and determination. I fought harder and refused to let others define me. Every step I took was fueled by a desire to prove the doubters wrong. But over time, I realized I was no longer living for myself. My decisions were driven by others' expectations, not my own dreams. The accomplishments felt hollow—they weren't truly mine.

I had become so focused on silencing the negative voices that I forgot to listen to my own. My victories weren't rooted in my own desires—they were driven by others' opinions.

Learning to Listen to My Own Voice

It took a long time to realize I had to stop proving myself to others. I had to learn to listen to my own voice—the one silenced beneath others' expectations. I began to ask myself: What do I want? What do I believe about myself? It was difficult at first, but slowly, I began to drown out the negative voices by focusing on proving to myself that I was right about who I was.

I realized that my worth wasn't contingent on others' approval—it was inherent. It was there all along, even when I doubted it. I didn't need to prove that I wasn't like my mother or that I wasn't just "the other child." I didn't need to prove anything to anyone.

The Power of Self-Belief

Self-belief is a powerful thing. It's the quiet confidence that comes from knowing who you are, embracing your worth, and choosing to live authentically. For me, it meant letting go of the need for validation. It meant recognizing that my value didn't come from my circumstances or accomplishments but from the person I chose to be every day.

When I began to listen to my own voice, I realized I was stronger than I knew. I had survived things that could have broken me, and I emerged with a newfound purpose. I was defined by my resilience and my ability to get back up, not by my past or mistakes.

The voices that once haunted me began to fade. They were replaced by a voice of love, compassion, and understanding— a voice that said, "You are enough, just as you are." It was no longer about proving anyone wrong but about proving to myself that I could live a meaningful and joyful life.

The Lesson: Prove Yourself Right

If there's one lesson I want you to take away, it's this: Stop trying to prove others wrong. Stop living your life by others' expectations. Instead, prove to yourself that you are right about who you are. Your value doesn't come from others; it comes from within.

There will always be people who doubt you, who judge you, who try to tell you who you are and what you're worth. But those voices are not your truth. You are the only one who can define your worth. You are enough, and you always have been.

Letting go of the need to prove others wrong was liberating. It allowed me to live for myself, to pursue what mattered to me, and to find joy in my journey. It allowed me to stop running from my past and start embracing my future.

Drowning Out the Voices

Drowning out the voices isn't about silencing them completely—it's about choosing not to let them control you. It's about finding your own voice, the one that speaks of your strength, resilience, and inherent value. The only voice that matters is your own. I had to learn to prove to myself that I was worthy, capable, and could rise above my circumstances to create a meaningful, joyful life.

If you've spent your life trying to prove others wrong, I encourage you to take a step back and listen to your own voice. Ask yourself: What do I want? What makes me feel alive and fulfilled? It's time to drown out the voices that say you aren't enough and start listening to the one that says you are.

Your journey is yours alone. Believe in your worth. Trust in your resilience. You are capable of achieving anything, not because others say you can't, but because you say you can.

As I let go of the need to prove myself to others, I am stepping into a new chapter—one defined by self-belief and authenticity. I am no longer running from my past or chasing validation. I am embracing who I am, flaws and all, and choosing to live a life that's true to me.

The voices of doubt may never disappear completely, but they no longer define me. My worth isn't determined by others' opinions; it's determined by who I choose to be. Today, I choose to believe in myself, to live authentically, and to be unafraid of living out loud, on my terms.

You have that same power within you!

> *Quote*
>
> *"Stop trying to prove others wrong. Instead, focus on proving to yourself that you are right about who you are. Your value doesn't come from the approval of others; it comes from within."*

Chapter 3

A Wandering Heart

I was born into a world that never stood still. You know what I mean—when life keeps moving before you even learn what stillness is. Before I could grasp the meaning of stability, I was already swept up by a tide of constant change. By the time I learned to remember the shape of a door, the color of a wall, or the scent of a neighborhood at dusk, it was already time to pack up and leave. Every six months, every year—off we went, leaving pieces of ourselves in places we would never return to, leaving behind memories scattered like broken puzzle pieces.

But let me tell you, the word "home" never sat quite right with me. How could it, when each so-called home was just another chapter that closed before I could even figure out the plot? These places were supposed to be sanctuaries, but they were simply stops on a journey that seemed endless. There was a pang of excitement in every new beginning—new walls to touch, new neighbors to meet—but deep down, behind every "new beginning" was a fear, a deep fear that we'd be uprooted before I could finally say, "This is where I belong."

I learned to live this way. To adapt, to accept, to keep going. But as a child, even beneath my smile, there was a knowing—

an understanding that something was missing. It wasn't until years later that I finally put a name to it: "roots". I wanted roots. I longed for the safety of belonging—somewhere, anywhere.

And then, for a moment, it seemed like my longing could come to an end. My mom married her first husband when I was still young. He wasn't my biological father, but he was everything I could've wanted in a dad. He showed up. He helped me with my homework, and he was there when I needed someone to lean on. It felt like magic—the stability I had craved my whole life. I let myself believe we were finally going to settle down, that this was it.

But you know, life has a way of reminding you that dreams are fragile. I remember the day it all fell apart. I walked into their bedroom, and there was my mother—her eyes blazing with a determination that terrified me. She was shoving his clothes into a garbage bag. And I didn't understand why. Panic consumed me. I tried to pull his clothes back out of that bag, tears streaming down my face, as if somehow, I could reverse what was happening if I could just put everything back in place. When that didn't work, I began to pack my own things, ready to leave with him. But my little plan fell apart, just like everything else.

That day marked the last time I remember feeling truly safe as a child. Even though he didn't leave that day, it was a reminder that one day he eventually would.

After he left, the illusion of stability left too. And what was left was chaos. Chaos became our unwanted guest—the constant, the familiar ache in the absence of what could have been a family. I was left in the aftermath, standing among the rubble, trying to make sense of a world that seemed indifferent to whether I had a place in it.

The moving never stopped—physically, emotionally. Each new marriage my mother entered into was a reset: hope, disappointment, rinse, repeat. She was searching for love, for connection, for a family that could heal the brokenness she carried. But with each new man, there was more instability, more confusion. My mother married three times before I turned thirteen, each marriage more turbulent than the last. And each one left its own mark, deepening the confusion I felt.

And then, there was my mother. My mother was a woman of contradictions. She loved me fiercely, she wanted to protect me, but her own pain was always right there, coloring everything she did. She often asked if anyone had touched me inappropriately, reminding me that my value was beyond what the world might see. She carried her own nightmares— violated, betrayed—and that distrust never let her fully let go. It made her love heavy, and sometimes, I felt more of her fear than her warmth.

In some strange way, it felt like a competition—me and my mom, competing against the men who entered our lives. She would bring them in, but the moment she felt a shift, she would retreat, leaving me feeling like an inconvenience. The relationships were fleeting, a revolving door of hopeful beginnings and bitter ends. The men came and went, but the weight of what they represented stayed—a reminder that love, for my mother, was like trying to grasp water with her hands. And I, her daughter, was caught in that current.

My friendships were fleeting, acquaintances more than bonds. I would arrive, and before long, I'd be gone. I learned not to get too close. Not to rely on anyone.

That disconnection didn't just affect my friendships. It grew inside me. Could I trust myself if no one stayed long enough to trust me? Could I be worthy of love if even those who promised to stay couldn't? I learned to expect people to leave before they had the chance to stay, and that expectation became my shield—my way of protecting myself from the pain of abandonment.

That emotional homelessness, it bled into every part of my life. My heart became a wandering heart—always seeking, never finding the stability it craved. I moved from job to job, apartment to apartment, relationship to relationship. To the outside world, it might have looked like I embraced change, but in reality, I was running.

Not toward anything, but away—from myself, from the fear that maybe I wasn't worthy of roots. Maybe I wasn't capable of building something that lasted.

But you know, fear is funny. It's both a prison and an invitation. One day, I chose to face it. To look back and understand where I'd come from, not to dwell but to heal. My wandering heart was searching for stability, yes, but also for courage. The courage to let go of the past, to believe that my history didn't have to define my future. And when I finally embraced that truth, I found that the power to belong had always been inside me.

It wasn't about the place—it was about me. It wasn't about staying still—it was about building a place within myself that was unshakable, no matter how many times the world shifted. A place where I could belong. And I realized that belonging isn't about the walls you live within; it's about the strength you build inside yourself.

And so, this wandering heart, it learned something. It learned that no matter where you are, no matter how many times you move, you can find a home within yourself. Because belonging, true belonging, starts from within.

> *"The journey wasn't about staying in one place—it was about finding a place within myself that I could trust, a foundation that wouldn't shake no matter how many times the world around me shifted."*

Chapter 4

Never Enough

Let me tell you something—not feeling good enough can be like a shadow. It seeps into every corner of your life, casting a dark veil over how you see yourself and how you engage with the world. It makes even the simplest moments feel like a test you're destined to fail. You overanalyze every word, terrified that what you say will somehow be wrong. You hold back, afraid to share your truth, because deep down, you believe it's not as valuable as someone else's. This fear becomes a barrier—one that keeps you from real, true, honest connections.

You start pleasing people, bending over backward to get the approval that never quite feels enough. That insecurity doesn't just affect your relationships—it's exhausting. It plays on repeat in your mind, replaying conversations, doubting your every move. Instead of showing up as your authentic self, you hide behind a mask, trying to be what you think others expect, all while feeling completely disconnected from who you really are.

I remember being nine years old, and my mom was getting ready to run some errands. I asked if I could come along, already expecting a "no" because that was always the answer. But this time, she said "yes." And let me tell you, I almost missed it. I was so used to hearing "no" that it took a moment for the "yes" to sink in. But when it did, it felt like a YESSSS in slow motion. I was excited—just running errands, but it felt like so much more. Moments like these were rare.

She told me to get dressed, and I ran to my room, picked out what I thought was the perfect outfit. I was ready, eager to go. But when she saw me, she just looked me up and down and said, "You're not wearing that." So, I rushed back, changed again, and still, the answer was the same. Not good enough. Panic set in. I threw clothes everywhere, desperate to find the perfect outfit. This was my last chance. I didn't want to be left behind. But I couldn't get it right. The answer came again, final this time: "You're not going anywhere with me looking like that. Just stay here."

I felt a pain that has stayed with me all these years. I wasn't enough. The tears were endless. I remember lying in a heap of clothes, crying until my head hurt, until my breath slowed. Looking back now, I think that was my first anxiety attack.

Later that same year, something similar happened. I was getting ready to go to church with my grandmother. I didn't have many clothes, but I picked the best I had. As we were about to leave, she said, "You're not going with me looking like that." No second chances that time. She left without me. And without realizing it, both my mom and grandmother planted a seed of rejection that I carried for years.

Fast forward. I'm married now—15 years into it. I'm getting dressed for dinner, changing my outfit over and over again, when my husband asks, "Why are you like this?" I looked at him, confused. "Every woman changes a million times before leaving the house," I said. He looked back and said, "Yeah, but you change a million times and end up right where you started. You looked good the first time."

That question stayed with me. It was something he'd asked before, but this time, something clicked. "Why am I like this?" I asked myself. And then, just like that, the memories came rushing in. I was nine years old again, feeling that same rejection, that same hurt. I cried, as if no time had passed. I was angry. I was angry with my mom. Why didn't she help me? Why did she expect so much from a child? And I promised myself right then that I'd never do that to my kids.

But then I realized, I was doing the same thing—just in a different way. I didn't leave them behind because of their clothes, but I made those little comments, like, "Are you wearing that?" or "Are you sure about that outfit?"

But my kids? They're different. They've got this confidence that amazes me. My son Isaiah, I asked him once if he planned to change because we had company coming over, and he looked at me and said, "Why would I change? I'm at home. I shouldn't have to be uncomfortable just because someone's coming over."

Another time, my youngest daughter came out of her room twirling around in a wild mix of patterns. I told her, "Your clothes don't match." She just looked at me and said, "I like them, and I'm happy." Who would argue with that? She was happy with herself.

And my son Trey—eighth grade graduation. He won multiple awards, including one for being "Most Likely to Be in a Presidential Position." It was a formal event, but Trey wanted to wear cargo shorts. I tried to convince him otherwise, even brought extra clothes just in case. But you know what? He stayed true to himself. He accepted four awards that day, and I sat there worried about what others thought of his outfit. Looking back, I regret not just enjoying the moment.

Even though I made those little comments, I always tried to instill in my kids the importance of being true to themselves. And I'm grateful they've embraced that lesson—even when it meant standing up to me.

I questioned myself for so long that I didn't even realize I was doing it. I haven't fully overcome those feelings of rejection, but I've made a promise to myself: I will wear what I want intentionally. I will invite others into my space without apologizing for what isn't perfect. And before I leave the house, I'll tell myself: You are enough. You look good enough. It doesn't matter what others think.

With my kids, I'm learning. I try not to judge their clothes, even if they're not what I would choose. Because I've realized, my concerns are more about what others will think than about what my children want or need. It's these little things that make a big difference. When our expectations are born out of our own traumas, they can hurt the ones closest to us.

Slowly, I've started letting go—letting them be true to themselves, just as I am learning to be true to myself. This realization didn't happen overnight. It came in pieces, in moments of reflection, in bits of self-awareness. And I began to understand—the instability in my life wasn't just external.

It was inside me. I had carried that chaos from my childhood, and it had become a part of me.

If I wanted to break free, I had to start from the inside. I had to take small steps toward healing—acknowledging the pain I had buried, feeling the emotions I had pushed down for so long. It wasn't easy. There were times when the weight of it all felt unbearable. But I knew I had to stop running. If I wanted stability, I had to find it within myself.

And so, I began the journey—step by step, day by day. Learning to trust myself, learning to love myself, and reminding myself every single day: I am enough.

> *"You are enough. You look good enough. It doesn't matter what others think."*

Chapter 5

When Love Feels Wrong

Before I even knew what love was supposed to be, I knew what fear was. My mother had a boyfriend—an abusive man, an alcoholic—who cast a shadow over our lives. He was the kind of man that made me feel small, made me shrink every time his eyes lingered on me. My mother? She was captivated by the idea of love, desperate for something that looked like stability in a world that felt chaotic. I could understand why she wanted to believe in him, why she needed that dream of normalcy. But the truth, my friends, is that there was nothing stable, nothing loving about this man. I felt the danger in my bones before anyone else did.

One weekend, he took us to visit his family. My mother, ever hopeful, thought it would be a good experience. But that weekend, it became a nightmare I could not escape. She decided I'd sleep in a room with his teenage nephews, believing they would treat me as a guest. But as darkness fell, the nightmare began. I remember their hands, believing I was asleep. I remember pretending I was asleep, hoping they would stop if I didn't react. But the hands did not stop.

I was a child—just a little girl—surrounded by older boys, outnumbered, powerless. They took turns, and in those silent hours, my innocence was stripped away. The next morning, I got up. I put on a smile, and I pretended nothing happened. But let me tell you, I felt like my body no longer belonged to me. I felt dirty, worthless, and completely disconnected from myself.

I wanted to tell my mother. I wanted to scream. But when I saw her smile, when I saw the happiness, she was trying so hard to hold onto, I chose silence. I chose to protect her happiness, even if it meant burying my own pain.

Now, as a child, I was a talker. I was that little girl who wanted to connect, to share, to be understood. But after that night, something in me shifted. I learned that speaking up didn't always keep you safe. Sometimes, the very people you turn to for comfort are the ones who hurt you the most. So, I retreated. Silence became my shield, my way of surviving. I stopped talking to others. Even with my mother, I began to hold back. I didn't want her to carry the weight of my pain.

The Impact of Silence on a Child's Mind

Silence does something to a child. It teaches you to carry burdens that were never meant for your small shoulders. It teaches you that your voice doesn't matter, that keeping quiet is the safest way to survive. But silence, let me tell you, does not mean peace. Inside, I was waging a war with myself. The longer I stayed quiet, the harder it became to find my voice again. I kept that night locked away, hoping that if I buried it deep enough, it would disappear. But trauma doesn't work that way. Trauma waits in the corners of your mind, seeping into your thoughts, into your behaviors, into the way you see yourself and the way you love.

Intimacy. A word that should bring warmth, connection, and trust. For me, intimacy was anything but that. It was a struggle, a reminder of the deep wounds I carried. When my husband looked at me with love, with admiration, I felt wrong. His gaze—though filled with nothing but affection—reminded me of those predatory eyes from my past. His touch, his tenderness, was met with a fear that I couldn't understand. I wanted to let him in, but instead, I found myself retreating behind walls I had built long ago.

I wasn't repulsed by him; I was repulsed by the parts of me that I couldn't reconcile. The shame, the fear, the disgust that lingered from those nights so long ago.

There were moments when my reactions were so intense that even I didn't understand them. He would reach out to kiss me, and I would recoil. Tears would fill my eyes, and I couldn't explain why. I could see the hurt in his eyes, the confusion, and it broke my heart. I wanted to be the wife he deserved, but I was haunted by ghosts that refused to let me go.

It took me years to realize that my reactions were not about my husband. They were about unhealed trauma. Those memories weren't just in my mind—they were in my body. Every touch I didn't want, every time I felt powerless, my body remembered. And every time my husband touched me; those memories resurfaced. If I wanted to experience true intimacy, I needed to face those ghosts. I needed to confront the trauma, to let go of the shame that had kept me imprisoned for so long.

Healing From the Wounds of Intimacy

Healing from trauma is not an easy journey, but it's a necessary one. It requires courage, vulnerability, and an openness to truly face the past. Here's what helped me heal:

1. Acknowledge the Pain

The first step was acknowledging the pain. I spent years pretending it didn't exist, hoping it would go away. But you can't heal from what you don't face. I had to admit what happened, accept that it wasn't my fault, and let go of the shame that wasn't mine to carry.

2. Seek Professional Support

Therapy was instrumental in my journey. It gave me a safe space to talk, to release what I had held inside for so long. My therapist helped me understand that my reactions were normal, that my body was trying to protect me. And understanding that helped me begin to separate the past from the present.

3. Communicate With Your Partner

Healing is not something you can do in isolation. I had to let my husband in. I had to share my story, to help him understand why I reacted the way I did. His love, his patience, his unwavering support became the foundation upon which I rebuilt my sense of intimacy.

4. Redefine Intimacy

Intimacy is not just physical—it is emotional, mental, and spiritual. I focused on building emotional intimacy with my husband. We talked, we laughed, we spent time together without the pressure of physical closeness. Slowly, I began to open up, and physical intimacy became something that felt safe and sacred.

5. Practice Self-Compassion

I had to learn to be kind to myself. I spent so long blaming myself for what happened, feeling ashamed of my reactions. I had to understand that my body was doing what it needed to survive. Self-compassion became my lifeline—a reminder that I was worthy of love, worthy of healing.

6. Create New Experiences

My husband and I began to create new, joyful experiences—cooking together, dancing in the living room, taking long walks. These simple moments helped replace the fear with new memories, memories of love, safety, and connection.

7. Release the Shame

Releasing the shame was perhaps the most powerful step. I realized that I was not defined by what happened to me. I was not broken; I was a survivor. And I was worthy of love, of intimacy, of joy. Letting go of that shame allowed me to embrace my husband's love, to receive it without fear.

Finding Freedom in Healing

The journey of healing is not a straight line. It's filled with setbacks and breakthroughs, moments of despair, and moments of hope. But every step is worth it. I found that true intimacy is about vulnerability. It's about allowing someone to see the parts of you that you're most afraid of, and finding the courage to let love in—even when it feels scary.

Today, I can look into my husband's eyes and see the love he has for me, and I can accept it. I can embrace it. Love, my friends, is not something to fear. It's something to cherish, something to nurture, something to hold close.

To anyone struggling with intimacy because of trauma, I want you to know—healing is possible. You are not broken. You are not defined by what happened to you. You are strong. You are deserving of love, of connection, of joy. It will take time, it will take courage, but step by step, you can reclaim your life. You are worthy of all the love this world has to offer, especially the love that allows you to be your truest self, in all its beautiful vulnerability.

> *"Healing is not about forgetting the past; it's about releasing its grip on you and reclaiming your power to love and be loved."*

Chapter 6

Who Am I

When I look back at my younger self, I see a young woman searching—searching for identity, for purpose, for stability. I was twenty-one, maybe twenty-two, living in Little Rock, finding my way in a world that felt overwhelming. It was during that time that I found The Watershed, a non-profit that was a lifeline to so many, including myself. And at the heart of it all was Reverend Hezekiah Stewart—a man whose impact was beyond words. Reverend Stewart was more than a leader; he was a force of good, a beacon of light for those who had lost their way.

I remember looking at him and thinking, if I could have chosen a father, it would have been someone like Reverend Stewart. He was a man who lived in integrity, who fought for those who had no fight left, who was a refuge for the lost. He became a role model, a symbol of the kind of person I hoped to be. I didn't have a clear idea of who I was then, but I knew I wanted to be more like him.

Reverend Stewart fought for single mothers who needed support. He paid utility bills for families on the verge of darkness, negotiated with utility companies when resources were scarce, fed the hungry, delivered furniture to those without, and advocated for education and employment.

He did whatever needed to be done. And in his presence, watching him give everything of himself, I began to feel a seed of purpose take root inside me. Though I didn't have the words for it back then, I felt it blooming.

Then came a moment that changed me forever. There was an organization, "Women and Children First," that was trying to move into a neighborhood in Little Rock. They provided emergency shelter for battered women and their children—women fleeing violence, looking for a new start. The need for a safe space was so great, and I was drawn to their mission. I understood what it was like to live in fear. I had seen my mother endure that fear, had watched her be broken by men who claimed to love her. As a mother myself, the thought of children facing that trauma broke my heart. I wanted to do something, even if it was just from afar.

Reverend Stewart was supposed to go to City Hall to speak on behalf of the shelter. But, like always, he was stretched thin—giving everything he had, every single day. And then he looked at me. He looked me in the eyes and said, "You should go. You can speak on behalf of The Watershed."

Me? I was stunned. I tried to tell him I wasn't ready, that I wasn't the right person for this. Public speaking wasn't something I had ever imagined doing—certainly not on behalf of battered women and children, not something so raw, so important. But he believed in me. He saw something in me that I hadn't yet seen in myself. And with that calm confidence, he said, "You'll be fine." And somehow, in that moment, I found myself believing him.

So, I went. I stood in front of City Hall, my heart pounding in my chest, my hands trembling. But then, I spoke. And what poured out of me wasn't rehearsed—it was my heart, my experiences, my deep care for those women and their children. I spoke about the importance of safety, the right to live without fear, and the opportunity to rebuild a life. And something incredible happened. I surprised myself. There was a power in my voice that I hadn't known was there.

When I finished, the room was silent for a moment. And then, the mayor—Mayor Dailey, I think it was—looked at me and asked, "Who are you?" There was no malice, no dismissal in his tone. It was genuine curiosity. I introduced myself again, told him I was representing The Watershed. But even as I left that day, his question stayed with me. Who are you?

That question echoed in my mind, and I realized I didn't truly have an answer. Who was I? I was a young mother. I was a volunteer. I was someone with a passion that I didn't yet fully understand. I was a woman who had been hurt, who had struggled, who was still finding her way. But in that moment, I also realized I was more than I thought. I had stepped up when I was needed. I had found my voice when it mattered. And I knew that this was part of who I was becoming. I wanted to help people.

I wanted to fight for those who couldn't fight for themselves, just like Reverend Stewart had done for me.

Reverend Stewart had a gift. He could see beauty in the midst of chaos. And maybe, for the first time, I began to see a glimpse of that beauty in myself. I was still struggling, still fighting to find my way. But now, I knew there was more to me. I was a young woman who wanted to be a voice for the voiceless, even if I was still learning to trust my own voice.

That day at City Hall, that moment of standing up for something greater than myself—that was a turning point. I may not have fully known who I was, but I knew who I wanted to be. And that was enough for me at the time. I watched Reverend Stewart pour himself into others, with so much love, so much dedication, and I thought to myself, one day, I want to be like that. Maybe not in the same way, but I wanted to leave that kind of mark on the world. I wanted to be the kind of person who could be a light for someone in their darkness.

Who am I?

Today, I can answer that question. I am a voice for the voiceless. I am an overcomer. I am a survivor. I am the boss of my own life—of my emotions, my actions, my reactions. I am living proof of what happens when you refuse to give up. I am an advocate for women, for those searching for their strength, for those trying to overcome their own mental barriers. I am a mother. I am a wife. I am a grandmother. I am a woman who has healed, but I am also a woman with broken pieces—pieces that will never quite fit back together. And that is okay. Those broken parts do not make me any less whole.

I am still becoming. And that, I think, is the most beautiful part of it all. The journey of becoming never ends. Every single day, I learn something new about myself, about who I am, about who I want to be. I am a work in progress, and I have come to love that process. The young woman who stood nervously at City Hall, unsure of her voice, is now a woman who knows her power. A woman who knows her story has meaning, and her voice can change the world.

Reverend Stewart taught me that you don't need to be perfect to make a difference. You just need to be willing. You need to show up, with all of your mess, all of your flaws, and be willing to stand for something bigger than yourself. That's what I strive to do. That is who I am—a woman who stands, who speaks, who loves deeply, who fights even when it's hard. I am becoming who I am meant to be, and that, my friends, is more than enough.

Claiming Your Name

If you're searching for your identity, if you're trying to claim your name, take intentional steps toward self-discovery and empowerment. Here are two ways to begin:

1. Embrace Self-Reflection and Honest Dialogue

Take time for honest self-reflection. Ask yourself the tough questions, and be open to hearing the answers. Journaling can be a powerful tool. Write down your dreams, your fears, your hopes, and your experiences. Reflect on the moments that have shaped you. Look at the stories you tell yourself and ask if those stories still serve you. Embrace a dialogue with yourself, and begin to see who you are beyond the expectations others have placed upon you.

Additionally, seek out meaningful conversations with those you trust. Find mentors, confidants—people who inspire you—and be open about your journey. Sometimes, others can help us see the parts of ourselves we overlook or undervalue.

2. Pursue Your Passions and Speak Your Truth

Discover what makes you come alive. Whether it's a creative hobby, a career path, a cause you care about— invest in it wholeheartedly. When you pursue your passions, you find parts of yourself you didn't know were there. Passions help you ignite your purpose; they bring clarity to who you are.

Speak your truth, even if your voice shakes. Sharing your thoughts, your experiences, and your values is essential to owning your story and claiming your name. Speaking your truth doesn't mean having all the answers—it means showing up authentically, even in the face of vulnerability. It's in that authenticity that you begin to carve out your true identity.

By embracing reflection, pursuing your passions, and speaking your truth, you can claim your name. You can step into who you are meant to be, and in doing so, find a strength, a purpose, and a joy that is uniquely yours.

"You don't have to be perfect to make a difference. You just have to be willing, and you just have to show up."

Chapter 7

Why Did I Say No

I went to school in Byhalia, Mississippi, a small town just outside of Memphis. Back in the '90s, it wasn't just the population that was small—it was the scope of our lives, our choices, our dreams. Life was simple, and sometimes, that simplicity came with struggle.

In our school, everyone got free lunch; it was just understood. No paperwork, no applications—it was the way we lived. Today, they call it the Community Eligibility Provision, a recognition of the schools serving the highest poverty areas. But back then, it was simply life—a quiet acknowledgment of where we stood, together, in our collective journey.

I remember one day; we were all gathered in the school gym. It was some kind of assembly, though I can't recall what for. What I do remember, what I can still hear in my mind, is the chanting. That chant that echoed off the walls, ridiculing families who received food stamps. We were just kids—middle schoolers—but the cruelty of that moment was as sharp as a blade. There is nothing quite as painful as the cruelty of children emboldened by a crowd. I sat there, and I knew I wasn't going to join in. I knew my boundaries. I wasn't going to be a hypocrite.

To my right, my friend was chanting the loudest of them all. Her voice carried above the others, and it stung me deeply. I knew her family received food stamps just like mine. Our parents lived in the same apartment complex. We had the same schedule for food stamp pick-up because our last names started with the same letter. I couldn't understand why she was pretending—why she was chanting, when she was just like the rest of us.

Then, I looked to my left. There was a girl, her head nearly in her lap, her face flushed with shame. She was trying to disappear, to become invisible, as if that might shield her from the mocking voices around us. Her mother worked in the school cafeteria, and she was one of the kindest girls I knew. Seeing her, trying to fold in on herself to hide from the cruelty, broke my heart.

I couldn't just sit there. So, I got up, walked over to her, and sat beside her. I wanted to say something that could take away her pain. I leaned in close and whispered, "Most of them get food stamps too." I wanted her to know she wasn't alone. She lifted her head, a flicker of hope in her eyes, and asked me, "Do you get food stamps too?"

And in that moment, I had a choice. And I chose wrong. Without hesitation, I said, "No."

I watched the light fade from her eyes, her posture collapsing back into the familiar shape of defeat. I knew, in that instant, I had made a mistake. I wanted to take it back. I wanted to say, "Yes, yes, I do. You're not alone. Please, don't feel this way." But it was too late. The moment was lost. I had let my own fear—fear of being exposed, fear of being judged—stand in the way of a genuine connection. And that choice weighed on me.

Even as a child, I knew I had messed up. I had let her down when she needed someone, and the worst part was that I hadn't even realized I was ashamed of receiving food stamps until that very moment. It was just life—a fact of my existence. I wasn't embarrassed until I was faced with the possibility of speaking it out loud. And that fear, that embarrassment, took hold of me and silenced the truth I wanted to share.

It Was a Trauma Response

Looking back now, I see it for what it was—a trauma response. Growing up in an environment where safety felt like it could be taken away at any moment, where love often came hand-in-hand with pain, I learned to protect myself. I learned to hold my truths close, because vulnerability felt like a risk I couldn't afford to take. I feared that if I shared my truth, it could be used against me—that even the girl sitting beside me, the one needing comfort, might one day turn around and use my vulnerability as a weapon.

Trauma shaped me into someone who chose safety over connection, who chose silence over truth. Deep down, I wanted to connect. I longed for relationships that were safe, where trust wasn't just a word but a reality. But the walls I built to protect myself also kept others out. Every time someone got too close, panic set in. The fear of being hurt again, the fear of abandonment, would take over, and I'd shut down. It wasn't that I didn't want love—I craved it desperately. I just didn't know how to let myself receive it without feeling exposed, without feeling like I was setting myself up for more pain.

That fear of exposure made my relationships difficult. I couldn't fully open up, couldn't trust that anyone would stay. I convinced myself I was better off alone, safer without the vulnerability of letting someone in. I had built walls that I thought protected me, but they were keeping me isolated from the very thing I needed most—connection.

I've had to learn how to trust again and again. And let me tell you, I've faced more setbacks than successes. Each time my trust was broken, it reinforced the idea that I was safer behind my walls. But deep down, I knew that wasn't the life I wanted. I wanted to be seen, to be known, to be loved for all that I am. So, I had to make a choice—a choice to risk the hurt, to let my guard down, to show up even when it scared me. And I learned that trust isn't something you give all at once. It's something you build—piece by piece, moment by moment—by showing up authentically, even when you feel terrified.

Seeing the Pattern

Why is this story relevant now? Because even as an adult, I see how those old fears still influence my actions. I see how sometimes, without even realizing it, I respond like that scared child I once was. I see how I hold back, how I hesitate when it comes to being vulnerable. I see how, even now, I sometimes lie—not outright, but by hiding my truth. It's a lie of omission, a lie born of fear. Somewhere along the way, someone betrayed my trust, and now, when I have a chance to connect deeply, I hesitate. I question if it's safe. I question if I can afford to let someone see me fully.

Our minds remember the hurt. They try to protect us, but in doing so, they often hold us back from the connections we crave. And we end up isolated, guarded, pretending to be something we're not, because we're too afraid to let the real parts of us be seen. And yes, we have to be wise—we have to be discerning about who we allow to see our most vulnerable parts. But if we truly want to make a difference, if we want to touch another person's life, it has to come from a place of authenticity. True change, true connection, can only happen when we show up as we are—flawed, imperfect, but real.

This fear—it shows up everywhere. In marriages, in friendships, in families. It shows up at work. We guard ourselves because we are afraid of getting hurt. But let me tell you, I am grateful that with my husband, we started as friends. That foundation allowed us to see each other without the weight of expectations. And even then, it took time—so much time—for me to let down my guard. But today, he knows me as well as I know myself. He knows every part of me—the good, the bad, the beautiful, and the broken—and he loves me just the same. And because of that, I can show up for him, and for myself, in all my authenticity, every single day.

Showing My Scars

So, what have I learned from all this? If I want to comfort someone, if I want to reach someone, I have to be willing to show them my scars. I have to let them see my "resume of demon-slaying," as I like to call it. YES, I have faced heartbreak. YES, I have been betrayed. YES, I am struggling right now. YES, I have financial problems. YES, YES, YES. Because if sharing my truth helps someone else stand a little taller, if it helps them change their posture from one of defeat to one of strength, then I will share it. I will not offer empty words. I will offer the raw truth of my life—because that is where real connection happens.

I wish I could go back and change my answer to that girl in the gym. I wish I could tell her, Yes, I get food stamps too. You're not alone. But I can't. What I can do is learn from that moment. I can be better. I can show up differently now. And that's what I choose to do—every single day.

> *"True connection comes when we have the courage to be vulnerable, to share our scars, and to say, 'Here I am, flaws and all.' That's where healing begins."*

Chapter 8

The Dream of Being Seen

I was only a child, around eight years old, when the dream began. A recurring vision that felt so vivid, it was more like a memory than something my imagination could have conjured. It was a cloudy Sunday afternoon, and church had just been dismissed. People were leaving in droves, and I found myself lost in that crowd.

But this wasn't an ordinary Sunday—it had the distinct feel of Easter Sunday, where everyone wore their finest pastel colors, their best smiles, as if celebrating the life and hope that the day represented. And then, just outside the church steps, there was this green buggy car, parked nearly blocking the stairs. No one else seemed to notice it, but I did.

I bent over, my curiosity leading me to peek through the window, and there, lying on the back seat, I saw a little girl. She looked just like me, dressed in the same Sunday best. I looked closer—and then it hit me—that little girl was me. I was in the car, lying there lifeless.

In that moment, I knew that I was dead.

I was having an out-of-body experience, and somehow, I knew I had drowned.

I felt desperation, an urge for someone—anyone—to notice that I was lying there, motionless. But the crowd kept moving, people walked past, and no one saw me. I felt the ache of invisibility as I screamed inside for someone to see me, to save me.

It's a dream that stayed with me, one that I remember as clearly now as I did when I was eight. I had it over and over again, though I can't recall for how long. It was just there, haunting the back of my mind.

And then I think back to when I was six years old, to an incident that might have set the stage for that dream. A well-meaning family member, believing the theory that a child thrown into the water would naturally float, tossed me in. But I was too old for that theory to work; instead of floating, I sank, struggling and terrified. I almost drowned that day.

Years later, as I grew and began to evaluate the meaning behind my dream, I noted three distinct things.

First-I was sure that I had drowned, but in the dream, there was no water. My lifeless body lay in the car, but there was no evidence of how I had ended up like that.

Second-no one saw me. Not a single person noticed that I was dead, lying there, and no one came to check on me. I was surrounded by people, yet I was entirely alone.

Third- The setting was church. Church was supposed to be my safe place, a place of refuge, and yet, even there, no one saw me.

The dream revealed so much more than my fear of water-it laid bare my deepest insecurities. It spoke to how I felt about my place in the world. I was traumatized by water, yes, but I was also haunted by feelings of invisibility, of being unloved, of feeling dead inside. Even in a place that was meant to represent safety and community, I felt unseen and unheard. I felt most alone when I was surrounded by people.

As I moved through life, those fears that had taken root in my childhood became patterns, affecting how I interacted with the world around me. Trauma has a way of doing that— of embedding itself so deeply that it quietly directs your actions, your reactions, without you even realizing it.

I remember one particular moment, years later, as a married woman. I was in the shower with my husband, and he playfully put water in my face. To him, it was harmless fun, but to me, it was something else entirely. I panicked, my body and mind thrown back to the terror of almost drowning as a child.

He didn't understand why I was "tripping over a little water," and honestly, at the time, neither did I. But the agitation I felt was real, and I couldn't shake it. I was angry with him for not knowing, for not understanding that something so small could hold so much power over me. But how could he understand when I didn't yet understand it myself?

This wasn't the first time. I remembered another moment, back when I was seventeen. I had just finished playing basketball, and I went to take a shower. A little water got in my face, and before I knew it, I was fighting against it as if I were drowning all over again. I had an anxiety attack right there in the shower. It made no sense to at the time, but I knew I didn't want to experience that again.

From that point on, I changed the way I showered, avoiding water in my face for almost ten years. And it wasn't until my husband challenged me that I realized just how much control that fear had over my life.

At twenty, I decided to confront my fear. I jumped into a swimming pool, determined to overcome it once and for all. But instead of swimming, I found myself sinking, panicking, and once again, almost drowning. My boyfriend at the time jumped in to save me, and I almost pulled him under with me in my panic. When he finally got me out, I remember thinking, "That's it. I'm never going to swim. It's just not for me." I resigned myself to being afraid.

Two years later, when I was twenty-two, I was at the pool with my children. Suddenly, one of them jumped into the deep end. Panic washed over me, and I looked around, desperate for someone to help. But there was no one. In that moment, I knew it was up to me.

I was terrified, but I thought, if I am ever going to swim, it will be now. I was ready to jump in—ready to risk it all—but just as I was about to, my son came up out of the water. He was fine. He could swim. Both my children could swim, thanks to lessons from my brother. They were fearless in the water, while I stood there paralyzed by my own fears.

Another moment stands out, years later, when we were living in Laguna Niguel, California. We were at the beach, and I decided I wouldn't let my fears keep me from enjoying my children. I grabbed their hands and started walking towards the ocean. But they pulled back, refusing to go any farther. It took me by surprise because they loved the water. Their father then came by, grabbed their hands, and they ran with him to the water without hesitation. That moment struck me deeply. They could sense my fear. They knew, without me saying a word, that I was scared, and they mirrored that fear. It was a powerful realization.

Water both terrified and fascinated me. I loved the ocean, its vastness, its mystery, but I feared its power over me. I've always been a dreamer, and I believe that my dreams are a form of divine communication. They've guided me, warned me, shown me paths to take, and water has always been central to those dreams. It was a symbol of both fear and renewal.

One of the most defining moments came when I was out on the water with my family. My husband and I were on a jet ski, while the kids were on a boat. I stood up to wave at them just as my husband made a turn, and we capsized. We were suddenly in the water, and for a brief moment, I felt my heart seize with terror. This was exactly what I had always been afraid of, and there I was, living it. But in that moment, something shifted. I thought, "No. I will not let this be the end. I will not die like this." My husband pulled me up from under the jet ski, and my son helped get a floatation device to me. I held onto the jet ski, surrounded by my family, and realized that I was fine. My worst fear had come true, and I had survived.

That experience was what I needed to finally break free. It solidified that I was not the same person anymore. I had faced my fear head-on, and it had not defeated me. I was fine, we were all fine, and I realized that I could let go of that fear. Today, I still cannot swim, but I can let water touch my face in the shower without panicking. I can go underwater without fear.

I can watch my children swim and not fear for their lives. And my favorite place to be is on the water—whether it's a lake, a river, or the ocean.

I was once so afraid of what water could do to me that I couldn't see what it could do for me. Water has always been my guide—at times terrifying, at times soothing. It has the power to destroy, yes, but also the power to cleanse, to renew, to give life.

Look back to discover what fears are holding you back so you can tackle them head-on. Often, what we most desire is on the other side of our deepest fear. I learned that I could be both scared and brave at the same time. My fear didn't have to define me. It could coexist with my courage, and I could still move forward. Today, I choose to embrace life fully, to face my fears, and to recognize that within the depths of those fears lies the potential for growth, freedom, and an entirely new beginning.

> *"True connection comes when we have the courage to be vulnerable, to share our scars, and to say, 'Here I am, flaws and all.' That's where healing begins."*

Chapter 9

Breaking the Cycle

Most of us are familiar with TikTok—whether we're sharing our stories or simply scrolling through the endless stream of creativity. It's an incredible platform, connecting people, bringing laughter, and sharing moments of humanity across the globe. But sometimes, beneath the humor, there lies a deeper truth—a story that reflects more than meets the eye.

I remember one particular day, scrolling through TikTok, when I came across a video titled "POV: My mom beating me for nothing." The video depicted a mother harshly disciplining her child, and eventually, the child rising up to grab the belt, declaring, "I'm not a small child anymore. You will not beat me anymore." It ended with the mother continuing to beat, kicking and punching until the child crumbled, crying in the corner.

At first, like thousands of others, I laughed. But something in me shifted as I watched it again. Suddenly, I felt sadness—an ache deep within my heart. Why were we laughing at this portrayal of abuse? Why were we finding humor in violence that, for so many, is all too real? The comments on the video were just as troubling. People joked, "If this ain't my momma" and "They did it because they loved us." They called it discipline, justifying actions that were anything but loving.

As a Black mother, seeing the hashtags like #blackmothers troubled me. It was perpetuating the stereotypes that have haunted our community for generations. It made me pause and think about how discipline—how trauma itself—has been normalized, even celebrated, in ways that harm us. So today, I want to share my reflections—*as a daughter, as a mother, and as a woman*—on the culture of discipline, the impact of generational trauma, and the power we have to break the cycle.

As a Daughter

Growing up, I began to understand that our parents—our mothers and fathers—were raised in survival mode. They were doing what they had been taught, using the tools they had, no matter how blunt or damaging those tools might be. My uncle once told me a story about my father, a story that shaped how I understood the way our people survived.

My father was an outspoken man, a quality that was both rare and dangerous for a Black man in Mississippi seventy years ago. He worked alongside his family as a sharecropper, a life built on the edge of fear and resilience. One day, my father talked back to the landowner, "the white man," as my uncle called him. My grandfather, terrified, tried to quiet him. But my father refused—he wouldn't stay silent in the face of injustice.

The landowner then turned to my grandfather and ordered him to beat my father—or else. He even dictated how—with a piece of wire, a light line. And so my grandfather complied. Not because he wanted to hurt his son, but because it was the only way he knew to keep him alive. It was an act of survival, a cruel necessity in a world that demanded submission from Black bodies.

Many of our parents grew up in those conditions. They raised us with that same fear, that same desperation. They would beat their children and say, "I'm doing this so the police don't beat you later." It was a twisted kind of love—a survival tactic meant to protect us from a world that didn't value our lives.

But here is the truth we must hold on to today: We are no longer living in survival mode. We have the power to change how we respond, to break the chains of generational trauma. I am not against discipline, but I am against abuse. There is a difference, a line we must recognize if we are to do better by our children. Just because it was done to us, does not make it right.

I remember coming home one day after spending the weekend with my stepfamily. My mother was furious—someone had told her that I had lied, that I said she let boys over, that she allowed me to go to clubs. None of it was true. I was only twelve. But my mother was triggered. She whipped me, yelling, "You know they already talk about me like a dog, and now you're lying on me?" I could see her tears, feel her pain. It wasn't about me. It was about her fear. Her own wounds spilling out uncontrollably. She rarely gave me a whipping and this was an unusual whipping; honestly an unusual response. She always gave me an opportunity to explain myself but her hurt caused her to be irrational.

As a Mother

When I became a mother, I made a conscious decision: I would not beat my children. I promised myself I would never spank them in anger. And I found that if I wasn't angry, I rarely felt the need to spank them at all. I chose consequences over punishment. Discipline that taught accountability, not fear.

Punishment, I learned, often had more to do with the parent's emotions—the anger, the frustration—than with teaching the child. So instead of punishing, I set consequences. I took away privileges, not as a way to control, but as a way to teach. And you know what? It worked. One day, one of my children asked me, "Why can't we just get a spanking instead of losing our things?" That's when I knew the lesson was taking root. Losing privileges made them reflect on their actions. It was a consequence, not a moment of anger.

But let me be honest—I wasn't perfect. I yelled. I said things I shouldn't have. My oldest daughter bore the brunt of my mistakes. I was only fourteen when I had her—we grew up together. There was one moment I will never forget. She had gone to a high school dance and paid for her boyfriend's ticket because he didn't have money. I lost it. I yelled, "Why would you do that? You don't want to end up like the women in our family, taking care of men."

My reaction was harsh, unfair. It wasn't until years later that I understood why. I had been nine years old, watching my mother buy an expensive pair of shoes for her boyfriend, while I sat terrified, wondering if we would have enough for school. My mother's actions had hurt me deeply. And when my daughter told me about paying for her boyfriend, it triggered that same fear, that same pain. It wasn't her I was yelling at—it was my past, my own unhealed wound.

As a Woman

Now, as a grown woman, I am determined to break the cycle. To end the generational trauma that has been passed down like an unwanted heirloom. I want to be conscious of my words, my actions, my reactions—and how they shape the lives of my children. I am committed to recognizing my own trauma responses and doing the work to heal. Because the truth is, healing doesn't just change your life—it changes the lives of generations yet to come.

When I watched that TikTok video, I saw how deeply abuse has been normalized in our culture. We laugh at it, we justify it, we call it discipline. But it's not discipline—it's trauma. And we have the power to stop it. We have the power to change, to heal, to create a different kind of legacy for our children. We no longer need to live in survival mode. We can create a path where our children are safe, where discipline doesn't mean breaking their spirit, but guiding them, allowing them to grow.

We have to be willing to look back—not to stay in the pain of the past, but to learn from it. To understand the fears that held our parents, the wounds that held us, and to be brave enough to break free. To create a world where our children thrive, not because they survived their childhoods, but because they were nurtured, supported, and loved.

Life, my friends, is not meant to be an endless uphill battle. We do not have to live our lives carrying the weight of our ancestors' fears and wounds. It is time to move from survival to thriving, from scarcity to abundance, from fear to freedom. It is time to break the cycles that have held us back and to heal from the trauma that has defined too many of our stories.

So let us be bold enough to choose love. Let us be courageous enough to choose healing. Let us be the generation that ends the cycle of fear and starts the legacy of wholeness. For our children. For ourselves. For every soul that follows. Because we are enough, just as we are—and we are capable of creating something better.

> *"You are not bound by the chains of your ancestors. You have the power to break them, to heal, and to create a new legacy of love and wholeness."*

Chapter 10

Understanding Triggers

Triggers can be defined as stimuli—whether sensory, situational, or emotional—that provoke intense reactions rooted in past experiences. These reactions often seem to come out of nowhere, feeling overwhelming and, at times, disproportionate to the situation at hand. For many women, especially those who have experienced trauma, triggers can dig up long-buried memories and emotions, leading to unexpected outbursts or emotional turmoil. It's as though a seemingly harmless sound, phrase, or gesture has the power to transport us back in time, to moments of deep pain, fear, or anxiety.

The difficulty in identifying triggers lies in their subtlety and the complexity of our emotional landscapes. Triggers are not always obvious, nor do they always make sense, but their effects are undeniable. The process of understanding triggers takes self-awareness, patience, and a willingness to look deeply into our own hearts, uncovering the sources of our pain and bringing them to the light

An Unexpected Trigger

Early in my marriage, I experienced a moment that brought the concept of triggers to the forefront of my awareness. It was a seemingly ordinary day, and my husband was eager to show me affection. He walked up behind me to give me a hug. Unbeknownst to him, I was lost in my thoughts, my mind wandering elsewhere, completely unaware of his approach. When he wrapped his arms around me from behind, I felt an instinctive jolt of fear. I spun around, yelling and crying, panic flooding my senses.

My husband stood there, stunned and confused, his eyes searching mine for an explanation. "What's wrong?" he asked, concern evident in his voice. But in that moment, I couldn't find the words to articulate what was happening inside me. All I knew was that I felt afraid, exposed, and suddenly very small. It was as though I was no longer in my own home, but instead transported back to a moment I couldn't quite place, filled with a fear I couldn't shake.

It took me time to process that moment. Initially, I blamed myself for overreacting. It was just a hug, I told myself. But as I sat with those feelings, I realized that it wasn't the hug that had upset me—it was the suddenness of it. It was the feeling of being caught off guard, of being touched unexpectedly, that triggered something deep within me. It took me back to a time when I often felt unprotected, when my body and my boundaries weren't respected, and when surprises often led to hurt or fear.

Understanding Triggers and Trauma Responses

That hug became a powerful moment of insight for me. It was the first time I truly understood how the experiences of my past had the power to influence my present—how the fears and vulnerabilities I carried from childhood could surface in the most unexpected ways. Triggers are not rational; they are not something we can simply "get over" or ignore. They are rooted in trauma, and until we take the time to understand their origins, they will continue to hold sway over our actions and emotions.

My reaction to my husband's hug was a trauma response—a deeply ingrained reaction shaped by years of feeling unsafe, unprotected, and unseen. Trauma responses are our mind's way of protecting us, but they often cause us to push

away the people we love, to build walls, and to live in constant vigilance, always waiting for the next moment of danger. My trigger was not about my husband's love or his intention; it was about my own internal struggle to feel safe and to allow myself to be vulnerable.

Lessons on Healing and Communication

Understanding this helped me communicate better with my husband. When I could finally articulate what I was feeling, I could help him understand that my reaction was not about him—it was about the unresolved pain I still carried. I explained that being touched unexpectedly could make me feel unsafe, even if it was from someone I trusted. And in sharing this, I opened the door for him to support me in a way that honored my boundaries and helped me feel secure.

Communication became a bridge between us. It allowed me to express my needs and fears, and it allowed him to understand me on a deeper level. It also helped me understand myself more deeply. Recognizing my triggers wasn't about blaming myself or feeling ashamed of my reactions; it was about giving myself grace and acknowledging that there was a reason for my feelings, even if I didn't fully understand them at the time.

Unpacking and Embracing Triggers

Triggers often manifest in subtle ways—ways that we may not even notice until we're overwhelmed by a sudden wave of emotion. Learning to recognize our triggers requires an immense amount of courage. It requires us to be honest with ourselves, to face the parts of our past that hurt the most, and to allow ourselves to be vulnerable, both with ourselves and with those we love.

If you are reading this and you feel that familiar pang of recognition, know that you are not alone. Triggers are a common experience, especially for those of us who carry the weight of past trauma. They are not a sign of weakness, nor do they mean that you are broken. They are signals— indications of areas in your life that need healing. They point to the wounds that still need tending, to the parts of yourself that are asking to be seen, heard, and understood.

There are steps you can take to understand your triggers and begin the process of healing. Keeping a trigger journal is one powerful tool—writing down your emotions when they arise, noting the situation, and reflecting on what you felt and why. Over time, patterns may emerge, helping you identify the specific experiences or stimuli that consistently provoke strong reactions.

Mindfulness can also help you stay grounded in the present, allowing you to observe your emotions without judgment and recognize the onset of a trigger before it takes over. Exploring the roots of your triggers through therapy or self-reflection can provide valuable context, helping you make sense of your emotional responses. And finally, open communication with trusted friends, family, or a partner can foster understanding and support, allowing others to help you navigate your triggers with empathy.

A Path Toward Healing

Unpacking and understanding triggers is an ongoing journey—one that requires patience, self-compassion, and a willingness to be vulnerable. It's about giving yourself permission to feel, to experience your emotions fully, and to acknowledge that those feelings are valid. Triggers do not define you, nor do they determine your worth. They are part of your story, but they are not the end of it.

By taking the time to understand your triggers, you begin the process of reclaiming your emotional landscape. You give yourself the power to respond with intention rather than react out of old wounds. Healing is not about never feeling triggered again; it's about learning to navigate those triggers with grace, about building a toolbox of coping strategies that help you feel safe, and about communicating openly with those you trust, allowing them to support you along the way.

Remember, dear reader, that you are more than the pain you have experienced. Your triggers are a part of your journey, but they do not define who you are. You are capable of healing, of growing, and of transforming that pain into something meaningful. Healing is about reclaiming your power, about choosing love over fear, and about recognizing that you are worthy of a life filled with peace, connection, and joy.

Healing is not a destination—it is a journey. It's a journey of understanding yourself more deeply, of honoring your past while embracing the limitless possibilities of your future. You are not alone, and with each step you take, you are moving closer to the freedom that comes from truly understanding your own heart.

Chapter 11

Weighted Gifts

Growing up, I often felt like an outsider in my own family. My siblings were the stars—they had gifts that could light up a room. They could sing like angels, harmonizing effortlessly while I sat on the side, mouthing the words. They could play instruments, making melodies that brought joy to everyone around them. They cooked meals that filled the home with warmth, did hair with such creativity it could rival a salon. And me? I couldn't do any of those things.

It wasn't their fault—my siblings were beautiful, talented people, and they never held their gifts over me. But I couldn't help the ache I felt as I watched them shine, while I stood in the shadows wondering why I hadn't been given the same glow. I questioned why God had left me out when He was passing out gifts. Why was I the one without a special talent? Why did it seem like everyone had something to offer except me?

I tried, oh how I tried. I wanted to sing, to be able to hit the notes that made others listen in awe. I tried cooking, hoping to find the magic my siblings had, but my meals lacked the spark that made people ask for seconds. I watched, I practiced, I tried to learn what came so naturally to them, but each time, I felt like I fell short. I felt like I was failing at something bigger than just a skill—I felt like I was failing at being me.

The Pain of Comparison

The truth is, when you spend your time measuring yourself against others, you lose sight of who you are. I was so busy comparing myself to my siblings that I couldn't see the person I was becoming. I couldn't see the unique light that was trying to break through all the self-doubt. The feeling of not fitting in, of being the odd one out, became my constant companion. It was like a shadow that followed me everywhere, whispering that I wasn't enough—that somehow, I was incomplete.

But comparison is a thief. It robs you of your peace, of your joy, and of your ability to see yourself clearly. My siblings weren't my competition; they were my family. They had their gifts, and I had mine. But it took me a long time to see it that way. I was so focused on what I couldn't do that I didn't realize what I could do. I was looking at their talents, their abilities, and missing the quiet, beautiful gifts that were blooming inside of me.

A Different Kind of Gift

The gifts I had weren't the kind that made people stand up and clap. They weren't the kind that filled a room with music or the aroma of a home-cooked meal. My gifts were quieter. They were the kind that you had to pay attention to in order to see. I had the gift of listening—the ability to truly hear someone's heart, to understand their fears and their hopes. I had the gift of empathy, of sitting with someone in their pain and holding space for them until the storm passed.

I had the gift of words, though I didn't recognize it at first. I couldn't sing, but I could speak in a way that connected with people. I could write, pouring my heart onto a page in ways that helped others feel seen and heard. My voice wasn't made for melodies—it was made for stories, for sharing my journey so others could find hope in theirs. These were gifts that took time to reveal themselves. They didn't shine brightly at first—they were more like embers, needing time and care to grow into a flame.

And the most important gift I had was resilience. Life had knocked me down more times than I could count, but I always got back up. I learned to stand on my own two feet, to find my way even when the path wasn't clear. That was a gift too—the strength to keep going when it felt like the world was telling me to stop.

The Beauty of Embracing My Own Journey

When I finally stopped trying to be like my siblings and started embracing who I was, everything changed. I stopped looking at what I couldn't do and started focusing on what I could. I realized that the world didn't need another singer, another cook, or another hairdresser. The world needed me— just as I was, with the gifts that were uniquely mine.

I started to see that my value wasn't in my ability to do what others could do—it was in my ability to do what only I could do. And that was powerful. I learned that comparison was a trap, and freedom came from embracing my journey, my gifts, and my purpose. I learned to honor my own path, even if it looked different from everyone else's.

It wasn't about shining brighter than anyone else. It was about shining in my own way. It was about understanding that my light didn't have to look like anyone else's to matter. I realized that every gift, every talent, every purpose was part of a bigger picture. And just because my role was different didn't make it any less important.

The Lesson: Celebrating Your Own Gifts

If there is one lesson, I want you to take from my story, it's this: Every single one of us has a gift, something that makes us uniquely ourselves. It might not look like the gifts of those around you, and that's okay. You weren't meant to be a copy of anyone else. You were meant to be you, in all your uniqueness, with all your beautiful differences.

It's easy to look at others and feel like you're missing something, like you're incomplete. But the truth is, you are complete just as you are. The gifts you have are exactly what this world needs. You don't have to sing to bring joy to others. You don't have to cook to create warmth in a home. Your gifts may be quieter, but they are no less powerful.

I have learned that my worth isn't tied to my ability to do what others can do. My worth is tied to who I am, to the gifts I carry that no one else does. And I have learned to celebrate that. I have learned to celebrate my siblings for their talents without diminishing my own. I have learned to honor my path, to let go of the need to compare, and to instead focus on becoming the best version of myself.

Finding Joy in My Unique Light

Today, I no longer feel left out of the blessings. I understand that God didn't skip over me when He was handing out gifts. He gave me what I needed to fulfill my purpose, and He gave my siblings what they needed to fulfill theirs. Each of us is here for a reason, and each of us has a light to shine. My light may not look like theirs, but it is mine, and it is enough.

I celebrate my gifts now—the ability to connect, to comfort, to inspire. I celebrate the gift of resilience, the gift of words, the gift of seeing others for who they are and helping them see themselves. And I celebrate the journey it took to get here, because every struggle, every moment of doubt, brought me closer to the truth of who I am.

So, if you've ever felt like you weren't gifted, like you were somehow left out, I want you to know that you weren't. You have gifts—beautiful, unique, powerful gifts. They may not look like what you see around you, but that's what makes them yours. Don't waste your time comparing your journey to anyone else's. Don't waste your energy trying to fit into someone else's mold.

Instead, honor the gifts that are uniquely yours. Find joy in your own light, and let it shine as brightly as it was always meant to. You are enough, just as you are, and the world needs the gifts that only you can bring.

> *"Everyone has a purpose, and every purpose has a path. It's when we honor our unique journey that we find the light we were always meant to shine."*
>
> —Oprah Winfrey

Chapter 12

Deep Betrayal

At twenty-three, I was living a life that was all too familiar. I had just delivered my fourth child, and once again, I was single, struggling to make it on my own. I was working two and a half jobs to keep a roof over our heads, barely seeing my kids as I dashed from one shift to another. We lived in a low-income apartment complex, and it was a time of relentless survival for me and my children. My son, so young and yet so resourceful, had even begun sweeping floors at the barbershop to buy food, all without my knowledge. He was carrying responsibilities no child should ever have to bear.

The apartment complex we lived in had strict rules. It was government-owned, and that meant no one was allowed to stay without prior approval. Every adult over the age of eighteen had to go through background checks, credit checks, proof of income—you name it. It was housing based on income, and the rules were firm.

During this time, my two younger brothers were living with my mom. They were adults, and they should have been on their own, but they were still with her, and that dynamic was unraveling. For reasons I still can't fully understand, my mother decided they could no longer stay. She turned them out, leaving them homeless.

I begged her to reconsider. I knew I had no space for them in my tiny apartment, and bringing them in would violate the rules and put me at risk of eviction. I pleaded because I was not in a position to take them in—but my mother refused. I felt the weight of it all—the unspoken expectation that, as always, I would be the one to step in. And so, I did what I thought I had to do. I took them in, despite knowing the risk. I felt responsible for my siblings, as I always had. It's what I knew. I had to be the one who showed up when no one else would.

But bringing them in was the beginning of a series of disasters I could have never foreseen. Twice, I came home from work to find notices on my door—warnings about unauthorized guests. I knew we were skating on thin ice. I went back to my mom, begged her again, explained that I was risking everything, that we would lose our home if she didn't help. She held her ground. She refused to take them back.

Looking back now, I know I should have let them figure it out for themselves. But I didn't. And eventually, the eviction notice came. My worst fears had become a reality. I had to start looking for a new place for me and my children—yet again uprooting the fragile stability we had worked so hard to maintain.

But that wasn't even the worst of it. The true betrayal was still ahead, waiting like a storm on the horizon.

One day, after another long shift at work, I walked through the door, and my daughter and niece were waiting for me. Their faces told me everything before they even spoke a word. I felt the weight of the room shift. It was as if time itself had slowed, and somehow, I knew—whatever they were about to tell me, it would shatter me.

They told me that the night before, both of my brothers had raped them. They weren't together. Neither of them knew the other was doing it. Somehow, on that same night, the ultimate betrayal happened—twice. How could such darkness exist within the very walls of my home? I still cannot wrap my mind around it. The pain was paralyzing. I felt the ground beneath me fall away, yet somehow, I stayed on my feet. I felt utterly betrayed by the very people I had taken in, the ones I had sacrificed so much for. They were my brothers—people I had loved, people I had stood up for—and they had hurt my family in the most unimaginable way.

I had worked so hard, fought so fiercely to protect my children from the kind of trauma I had endured as a child, only to unknowingly invite it into my own home. How could I have known? How could I have imagined that those I loved most would be the ones to cause the greatest harm?

Despite the shock and devastation, I had to stay strong for the girls. I took them to the hospital to confirm their stories. I filed a police report. I had my brothers arrested. I remember the confusion from other family members—How could you do this? They are your brothers. But I was equally confused— How could I not?

I come from a family that has long believed in keeping our pain in the shadows, in keeping secrets, in keeping "the family business" private. But that secrecy—oh, that silence—

had allowed darkness to persist for too long. I knew I had a choice to make: protect my brothers, or protect the girls. And I chose the girls. Because enough was enough. Generations of women in our family had been violated by those who should have protected them. And I decided it was time for a change. It was time to bring what was hidden into the light. It was time to say no more.

The consequences were staggering. I stood by the charges. My youngest brother, spent the rest of his life in jail, dying at twenty-six. And I loved him dearly, despite everything. My older brother spent sixteen years in prison. He never forgave me. He never understood why I did what I did. But I knew— I did it for the girls. I did it because that was what was right.

I had no family support. My mom seemed to understand, but it was a lonely road. The weight of the trauma, the betrayal, the loss—it felt suffocating. I carried guilt. I carried shame. And I carried the burden of what had happened in our home.

I remember going to work at the Embassy Suites Hotel in Little Rock, trying to get through my shifts without breaking down. I overheard a coworker reading from the newspaper— he was reading an article about my brothers. He read it aloud, mocking them, calling them "trailer trash." He didn't know they were my family. I quietly walked to the restroom, dried my tears, and came back to finish my shift.

The betrayal, the pain, the resentment, the guilt, the loneliness—it was all there, wrapped around me like a shroud. And now, there was embarrassment too. How does one heal from that? How do you move forward after such a deep wound? How do you find God in the midst of such pain, when you've done everything, you could to help others, only to be hurt in return?

The Stages of My Healing

1. Forgiving Myself

I blamed myself for working so much, for not being there. But who else would have provided for us? I did what I had to do, and I had to forgive myself for that.

2. Forgiving My Mother

I blamed my mother for making her children my responsibility. I had to forgive her too, to let go of the anger I felt for the position I felt she put me in.

3. Giving My Daughter Back to God

I didn't know if this would make her stronger or break her. Sexual abuse had been part of what made me stronger, but it had nearly broken my mother. I had to release my daughter to God and trust in her resilience.

4. Letting Go of Responsibility for My Brothers

They made a choice, and I had to remind myself that their actions were not my responsibility. They chose to harm, and it was their responsibility to do the right thing—not mine to fix their wrongs.

5. Accepting the Guilt, But Not the Shame

Guilt was part of the process. I had to admit my mistakes. But shame belongs to those who violated my trust. I had to return that shame to its rightful owner.

6. Admitting I Messed Up

I made a mistake by letting my brothers in. No matter how much I wanted to help, my kids should have been my priority. I admitted it out loud—I messed up.

7. Apologizing

I apologized to my daughter and my niece. I told them it was not their fault, that they were victims. I made sure they knew I was sorry for not protecting them.

8. Taking Care of Myself

I had to care for myself—mentally, physically, spiritually. I had to make a conscious decision not to dwell on the pain. To find light, even in the darkest times.

10. Being Patient

Healing takes time. You cannot rush it. The kind of trauma we faced doesn't simply disappear. I learned to be patient with myself, to understand that even when I thought I had moved past it, triggers would come. And when they did, I reminded myself—I am still healing.

I wish there were an easy way to get past this kind of pain. I wish there were a quick fix, a way to make everything better overnight. But I've learned that true healing is about choosing, every single day, to move forward. It's about offering yourself grace, even when it feels impossible. It's about believing that, despite everything, you are still worthy of love, still capable of joy.

"Forgiveness is giving up the hope that the past could have been any different."

—Oprah Winfrey

Chapter 13

Intimidation to Inspiration

There was a time when seeing a strong, healed, passionate woman would stir something inside of me, and it wasn't inspiration. I would watch these women—glowing in their relationships, thriving in their careers, comfortable and powerful in their own skin—and instead of feeling empowered, I felt intimidated. I felt small. And I felt envious.

My first instinct was to tell myself a story about who they were and, more importantly, how they must see me.

They think they're better than me.

They must see every flaw I have.

I don't belong in their presence.

And so I would shrink. I would withdraw, convinced that I wasn't good enough to stand beside them. I blamed them for the way I felt about myself, as though their strength somehow magnified my own perceived weaknesses. These women became mirrors I avoided, because I feared the reflection that I'd see.

Isn't it peculiar? To admire someone deeply and yet be afraid of them at the same time. I admired these women, but that admiration twisted itself into resentment, because I didn't believe I could ever be like them. And so I chose to stay small, hidden in the safety of my own insecurities, where no one could see my vulnerability.

But here's what changed—whether through a gradual awakening or a sudden realization—I came to understand that the discomfort I felt had nothing to do with them and everything to do with me. The truth was, I saw in them the very things I wanted for myself. Their energy, their grace, their unwavering confidence—it was not something to fear; it was something I longed for. And the real work began when I decided to lean in rather than pull away.

I learned to move closer to the very things that intimidated me. Because growth, my friends, does not happen in our comfort zones. Growth happens when we step into the spaces that make us uneasy, when we choose to be around the kind of people who reflect back the best parts of what we aspire to be. I began to see these women differently—not as threats, but as reminders of what was possible for me.

They were showing me what I could be, what I could become.

It was not easy. Vulnerability is uncomfortable. It asks you to confront the parts of yourself you'd rather ignore. But when I allowed myself to lean in, I found something truly transformative: those women who once intimidated me were also the ones who lifted me up. They weren't looking at me with judgment. They weren't picking apart my flaws. They were cheering for me. They wanted me to succeed, to grow, to shine.

And that, right there, was the turning point.

I realized that these are the kind of people you want in your corner. People who hold the energy of growth, of healing, of passion. When you surround yourself with those who are thriving, something remarkable happens—you begin to thrive too. You learn by witnessing their courage, by feeling the warmth of their joy, by watching how they navigate the world with grace. Their success doesn't diminish yours; it enhances it. Their light doesn't cast a shadow over you—it shows you how brightly you, too, can shine.

There is enough light for all of us, and I learned to stop hiding from that truth. Instead of letting someone else's glow make me feel small, I let it warm me, let it inspire me. I changed the narrative from I am not enough to I am worthy. Worthy of standing here, worthy of being seen, worthy of growing, worthy of thriving.

As I leaned into this new way of thinking, something beautiful happened. The qualities I admired in others, the very things that once intimidated me, I began to see in myself. I could be strong. I could be healed. I could be passionate. I could celebrate the success of another woman without feeling like it diminished my own value. I realized that these powerful women were not my competition—they were my allies. They were my sisters on this journey of becoming.

So, here's to the women who inspire us, who make us want to be better, who challenge us to grow. Here's to the ones who shine so brightly that they help us see our own light. Here's to those who walk with grace and strength, reminding us, by their very presence, of what is possible.

We grow by stepping into the spaces that make us uncomfortable. We flourish when we surround ourselves with those who elevate us. We rise, not by hiding in the shadows, but by stepping fully into the light of our own potential.

Lean into the light. Let it reveal who you are meant to be. Let the success of others be the fuel that pushes you forward, not the reason you hold back. Remember, there is room for all of us to shine. And when we shine together, we are unstoppable.

> *"The more you praise and celebrate your life, the more there is in life to celebrate."*
>
> **—Oprah Winfrey**

Chapter 14

Feeling Unworthy

When I was about eleven or twelve years old, my mother had a new boyfriend, and she was preparing to meet his family for the first time. I wanted so badly to go with her. I remember begging her, pleading with every ounce of my heart, even trying to strike a deal in my childish way. But no amount of persuasion worked. In the end, she said no, and I had to stay behind. Disappointed? Absolutely. But I thought I had moved on. I thought I had let it go.

Fast forward to her next visit to his family, and this time, she decided to take me along. I was excited—I felt like it was my chance to belong, to be part of whatever this new chapter meant for her. I remember walking into that house with a sense of hope. And then, the aunt looked at me with confusion, her eyes narrowing as she asked, "This isn't your daughter, is it?" My mother, a little uncomfortable, confirmed, "Yes, she is." The woman wouldn't let it go, saying, "But you brought a different daughter last time." I stood there, frozen, the words sinking in slowly, painfully. My mother eventually explained that she had brought my cousin the first time.

And I stayed silent—but inside, I was unraveling. I felt like the ground beneath me had shifted. The hurt that washed over me was deep, raw, and inescapable. Why would she take someone else and pretend they were hers? It was a question that gnawed at me. Was my mother ashamed of me? Was I not enough? My cousin, with her lighter skin, her beautiful hair, her perfect smile—she was the one my mother chose. And in that moment, the belief that had haunted me for years—that I was somehow less than, somehow unworthy—came crashing down on me with an intensity I couldn't fight off.

That small moment carried a weight that I would carry for decades. It broke something in me that day—something fragile, something I hadn't even realized was vulnerable. For years, I couldn't tell this story without tears. It seemed so small, but it was a tiny crack that let every insecurity spill out. It was trauma—a wound that festered because it seemed to confirm everything I had feared. I wasn't enough. I was never enough.

But time, if we let it, has a way of bringing us closer to truth and healing. In my late thirties, my mother and I finally talked about it. Really talked. She took responsibility for her actions—she acknowledged my pain and asked for forgiveness. And that simple acknowledgment, that willingness to see me and my hurt, brought healing in a way I had never imagined. It didn't erase the pain, but it began to soothe it. It reminded me that sometimes, the healing we need comes from being seen, from having our hurt recognized and held. This experience taught me that the seemingly insignificant moments in childhood can shape us, can leave us with wounds we carry far into adulthood—wounds that only honesty and courage can begin to heal.

How Rejection Manifested in My Adult Life

Rejection doesn't stay confined to our childhoods. It has this sneaky way of showing up when we least expect it, even in the smallest of moments. I remember one time, as an adult, when my best friend asked me to help decorate for her dad's birthday party. I was excited to help. I showed up with suggestions and enthusiasm. And in the end, she chose the recommendations of another friend. Objectively, I could see that their idea was better—of course it was better. But it didn't stop that wave of rejection from crashing over me.

It wasn't about the decorations. It wasn't about whose suggestion was better. It was about that old wound being reopened, that familiar feeling of not being enough making its unwelcome return. And without even realizing it, I shut down. I withdrew. I pulled back, not because of what was happening in that moment, but because of what that moment triggered from my past.

I eventually talked to her about it, apologizing for my withdrawal. I knew she probably had no idea why it mattered so much—why it hurt so deeply. And honestly, looking back, it shouldn't have. But that's what unhealed pain does. It sneaks in through the smallest cracks, threatening to pull you away from what could be beautiful relationships.

The truth is, rejection is a powerful force—it lingers long after the moment has passed, coloring our interactions and shaping our responses in ways we don't always realize. It convinces us, in those quiet moments of doubt, that we are unworthy, unseen, or forgotten. But as I've learned, acknowledging that pain is the first step toward breaking its hold. It's not about erasing the past or pretending those moments of hurt didn't happen. Instead, it's about recognizing the patterns they've created in our lives and choosing to address them.

For so long, I let those old wounds dictate how I showed up in relationships, in my own life. I let them shrink me, silence me, and make me feel small. But healing doesn't come from ignoring the cracks. It comes from facing them head-on, from having the courage to voice our pain, and from giving ourselves the grace to accept that our value was never determined by someone else's choice.

In those moments when rejection rears its ugly head, I remind myself of the truth that took decades to accept: I am enough. I always have been. And while the past may have shaped me, it no longer defines me. The power lies in how I choose to move forward, in how I allow myself to heal, to grow, and to love—starting with loving myself fully, even in the places where I once felt broken.

> *"When you undervalue what you do, the world will undervalue who you are. But when you see the power in others as a reflection of your own potential, you begin to rise. Let us celebrate the light in one another, and by doing so, let our own light shine even brighter."*
>
> —Oprah Winfrey

Chapter 15

Embracing a New Love

I wasn't someone who came to physical affection naturally. Touch, closeness, and cuddles were not the language of love in my upbringing. In our home, love wasn't spoken through lingering hugs or gentle caresses; instead, it was in the unspoken sacrifices, the food on the table, the clothes that kept us warm. I didn't grow up knowing how to hold someone, how to let someone hold me. And because of that, love stayed in my mind, but rarely did it make its way to my fingertips.

But then I had my own children. I found myself in a new space—a space filled with little hands that reached for me, arms that wrapped around my waist, tiny voices that wanted comfort not only in words, but in touch. My children craved hugs, closeness, connection. And there I stood, with all my love for them, realizing I had no idea how to give it in the way they needed.

It was easier with my sons. Somehow, culturally, it felt more acceptable, more natural, to hold them close, to offer protection through touch. With my daughters, there was an emotional distance I hadn't even realized was there—a distance that was about the way I had learned to be, the way

I had been taught to survive. And then there was my youngest daughter—the most affectionate of all. She reached for me constantly. She needed that closeness, that touch, and I found myself struggling to give her what she so freely asked for.

There came a moment when I realized something had to change. I could feel the gap between what they needed and what I was giving. And that realization broke me open, because it showed me a version of myself I hadn't known before—a mother who wanted to meet her children exactly where they were. So, I made a choice. I chose to be honest. I sat my kids down and told them, "This is hard for me, but I love you enough to learn."

We came up with a plan. We started with small, manageable steps. Short hugs—just a few seconds at first. We practiced together, and each time, those brief embraces grew longer, became more natural, more comfortable. And in time, I found myself leaning in, not just physically, but with my heart. What began as a conscious effort, an uncomfortable learning curve, blossomed into something beautiful. Today, I am the one who reaches for them first. I am the one who wraps them in my arms and holds on, not because I have to, but because it has become as much a part of me as breathing.

Reflecting on why this journey felt so foreign led me to look back, to examine my cultural history. In the history of Black families, there has often been a complex relationship with physical affection. Generationally, we were conditioned to hold our sons close, to love them tenderly and protectively, out of a fear born of history—a fear that we might lose them. That love was expressed with every hug, every touch, every time we pulled them in close to our bodies, as if we could shield them from the world.

Daughters, on the other hand, were raised with a different kind of love—one forged in strength, in resilience, in survival. We taught them independence, toughness, because we needed them to be ready for a world that would test them. The love wasn't any less real, but it was expressed in ways that were different.

When I realized how this history lived in me, it all made sense. I understood why I held back, why physical affection didn't feel instinctive. But I also knew I wanted more for my children. I wanted to expand, to give them the love they deserved in all the ways they needed. I wanted to show them that love isn't confined by what we've known. Love grows. Love stretches us. And sometimes, love asks us to move beyond the boundaries we've set for ourselves.

Today, I am no longer the mother who hesitates to reach for her children. Touch, closeness, affection—they are as much a part of our family as laughter, as tears, as every moment we share together. And I realize now that it was never about becoming someone else—it was about discovering a part of myself that had always been there, just waiting to be uncovered.

Love is not fixed. It isn't limited by what we've known or where we come from. It's a living, breathing thing that grows, that expands, that transforms. And in learning to embrace my children fully, I discovered a deeper love for myself too. I realized that there is always room for growth, always room to learn a new kind of love.

So, here's what I've learned: Love can be learned. It can be taught, it can be practiced, and it can be transformed into something more beautiful than you ever thought possible. It's about stepping into the discomfort, about being willing to grow, about opening up to the possibility of something more.

Love is not limited by our past. Love has no bounds except those we put on it. And when we let go of those limits, we make space for deeper connection, for greater intimacy, for the kind of love that holds on, and never lets go.

> *"Love is a process of learning, of unlearning, and of expanding beyond the comfort zones we were taught to stay in."*
>
> —*Oprah Winfrey*

Chapter 16

The Need to Please

"**P**ick up your clothes, vacuum your bedroom floors, and make sure everything is put away," I reminded the kids, my voice hurried, as if each instruction was a lifeline holding back chaos. I moved from room to room, my eyes sweeping every surface, making sure every single thing had its place.

"What are you doing?" my husband asked, looking at me with that blend of curiosity and confusion that had become all too familiar. Without missing a beat, I replied, "What does it look like? I'm cleaning! It's Tuesday, and the housekeeper will be here any minute." He shook his head, watching me dart around. "I don't get it—you always clean before the cleaner arrives. It doesn't make sense."

But to me, it made all the sense in the world. How could I let someone into my home if it wasn't in order? How could I bear for someone—even a housekeeper—to see the mess, the bits of life that piled up when I couldn't keep up? Toys scattered, dishes that hadn't been put away, laundry that was still waiting for its turn. I needed her to see a version of me that was put together, a version I often struggled to embody even for myself.

It struck me then, as I rushed around, that I wasn't just tidying up for a housekeeper. I was cleaning because I was desperate for her approval, for her silent nod that said, "You've got it together." I hired her to help me, and yet I feared she'd see my shortcomings. My need for validation was so deeply rooted that even the presence of someone who was there to take care of the disorder made me feel like I had to prove something. I was afraid of what she might think— afraid that, even in her role, she might judge me. And that fear was always there, lurking, convincing me that I had to be someone else, someone flawless.

I walked through the dining room and noticed the tablecloth was hanging unevenly. I called to my daughter, "Straighten up the tablecloths—one side is longer than the other. I don't want people thinking I don't pay attention to detail." It seemed insignificant to her, something she could hardly notice. But to me, that tablecloth was a reflection of competence, a sign that I was in control.

I moved towards the garage door. It was open, exposing the bins, the half-finished projects, the tools. "Close the garage door, please," I called out, not able to bear the thought of someone seeing that mess. "I don't want that to be the first thing people see." What if the neighbors drove by and saw it? What if they thought this chaos was a reflection of who I was—disorganized, out of control, incomplete?

Every part of my life felt like a stage where I had to manage appearances. It wasn't just about the housekeeper, the neighbors, or the guests—I realized it was about managing how *everyone* saw me. I wanted people to think I had it together. I wanted the details to be perfect because, deep down, I believed that was the only way I could feel worthy.

The clean house, the perfectly set table, the closed garage door—all of it felt like it held the key to my value.

And yet, no matter how much effort I put in, it never felt like enough. I was exhausted, always performing, always trying to control how others perceived me. I needed them to think well of me, needed them to see me as capable, organized, competent—because I struggled to see those things in myself. I believed if everything around

me looked perfect, then maybe, just maybe, I could finally be worthy of the love, respect, and praise I longed for.

People-pleasing was my way of avoiding rejection. It was my way of trying to outrun the voice in my head that whispered, You're not enough. And in order to quiet that voice, I sacrificed my comfort, my authenticity, my own peace of mind. I became obsessed with curating a version of myself that would be deemed acceptable by everyone else, all the while ignoring the truth of who I was beneath the surface.

But here's the reality: no amount of tidying up, no level of perfection, could ever fill the gap that existed within me. All that effort—all those hours spent making sure everything was just right—never quieted the part of me that doubted my own value. The need to people-please was never about impressing others; it was about masking the deep-rooted insecurity that made me feel unworthy of love just as I was.

And one day, I had to ask myself: When will I finally be enough? When will I allow myself to let go of all the performances and just be?

The truth I came to learn, and the truth I'm still learning every day, is that real worth has nothing to do with what other people see, and everything to do with how you see yourself. It's not about how neat the house is or how perfect everything looks; it's about knowing, at the end of the day, that who you are is enough. It's about realizing that you don't need anyone's approval to be worthy, and that your value is not something you have to earn through performance.

People-pleasing is exhausting because it asks us to prove what's already true—that we are worthy. And when I let go of that desperate need to control how others saw me, when I allowed myself to be real, to be seen as I am—that's when I found peace. That's when I started living for myself, not for the fleeting nods of approval from others.

Letting go of people-pleasing is not a one-time event. It's a daily choice to remind yourself that you are enough as you are. It's choosing authenticity over perfection, peace over performance. And it's allowing the mess, the imperfections, the parts of your life that aren't always picture-perfect, to just be—because you are worthy, not because of what you do or how well you perform, but because of who you are. And that is more than enough.

> *"When you let go of what people think and live in the truth of who you are, you free yourself to live with genuine joy."*
>
> —Oprah Winfrey

Chapter 17

Beyond The Closet Door

When I was a young girl, I spent a weekend with a caretaker, surrounded by other children. We ran outside, played games, and it was supposed to be one of those weekends where the innocence of childhood felt boundless. But sometimes, the smallest of things can have the most profound impact.

I remember it clearly: one afternoon, we were playing in the carport, and somehow, a scratch ended up on the wall. It wasn't anything significant, just a mark that none of us truly knew how it got there. But before long, fingers pointed in my direction, and I was the one who got the blame. I recall the caretaker's anger—it was far beyond anything I had imagined for such a small offense. Her response was swift and severe. She tied my hands behind my back and placed me in a dark closet.

I can still feel it—the cold wave of fear that rushed over me, how my heart pounded louder with each passing second as the door shut, plunging me into darkness. My young mind could barely grasp what was happening. All I knew was that I felt utterly trapped. The world shrank into that tiny space, into the suffocating darkness, with my hands bound, the air thick with dust and terror. It was a moment that lasted for what felt like forever. And even though I eventually left that closet, the fear stayed with me.

From that day forward, enclosed spaces became my nightmare. Claustrophobia, yes—but it was more than that. It was the memory of being powerless, the lingering impact of that moment of fear and isolation. It dictated my life for years. Elevators? I'd take the stairs. Closed rooms? I needed a window or an open door. Planes? Out of the question. It was as though the world around me had become a series of locked closets, all waiting to close me in again.

Years later, I finally began to understand it for what it was—not just a fear, but a trauma response. Therapy allowed me to revisit that dark place—not in body, but in spirit. I had to face that darkness again, had to acknowledge the fear that had lived within me for so long. It wasn't easy. In fact, it was one of the hardest things I've ever done. The resistance was overwhelming, as if opening the door to that memory would leave me once again powerless. But deep down, I knew that I could not let it hold me anymore. I knew that, in order to truly live, I had to find a way to open the door from the inside.

And then there came a pivotal moment—a moment that called me to take a leap of faith, literally and figuratively. An opportunity came for me to fly to California. To get on a plane. The very thought of it made my chest tighten. It was as if every fear, every moment of feeling trapped, was conspiring to keep me on the ground. But there was another feeling—a pull, a whisper of something greater. It was the spirit of God nudging me out of my comfort zone, inviting me to trust, to take a step in faith.

So, I did. I stepped onto that plane, my heart pounding, my hands trembling, my breath coming in shallow waves. I prayed with every beat of my heart, holding on to the belief that I was being led for a purpose. And that flight—the one that terrified me—ended up taking me toward the greatest blessing of my life. It was on that trip that I met my husband, my partner, the love of my life. And in that moment, I realized: what if I hadn't taken that step? What if I had let fear dictate my decisions? What if I had missed out on the love of my life because I was too afraid to face a trauma that had held me captive for so long?

It taught me a lesson that I carry with me every day: There is always something on the other side of fear. Fear often stems from a moment in our past—a moment where we felt broken, powerless, trapped. Fear tries to convince us that we are still that scared, helpless version of ourselves, that the darkness is still looming. But the truth is, the door that once trapped us is no longer locked. We have the power to open it, to step through, and to find freedom on the other side.

The Lesson: Faith Steps in Overcoming Trauma

As I have said many times already, healing from trauma is not a straight path. It requires steps of faith, and each one challenges the fear that keeps us small. Every step we take brings us closer to reclaiming our power, closer to the truth that we are not the helpless children we once were.

Here are some of the lessons I learned along the way:

1. Acknowledge the Source

Trauma often lurks behind fears that seem irrational. It took therapy for me to trace the roots of my claustrophobia to that closet. Acknowledging where the fear came from allowed me to understand it and begin the healing process.

2. Take Small Steps

Healing doesn't happen overnight. It comes in small, deliberate steps. Therapy was my first step. The next was slowly challenging myself to face enclosed spaces—a little bit at a time—until finally, I boarded that plane. Each step, no matter how small, was a victory that led to the next.

3. Listen to the Voice of Faith

Fear will always try to keep you where you are, but there's another voice that speaks, even if in a whisper. The voice of faith. It encourages us to take a step, even when we're scared. It tells us that there's something more waiting for us. It's that quiet urging that pushed me to fly to California, that told me there was more for me on the other side of fear.

4. Trust That There's a Blessing on the Other Side.

What if your greatest blessing lies beyond your greatest fear? Had I let fear keep me grounded, I would have missed out on the most beautiful part of my life. Facing trauma is never easy, but the freedom, the love, the unexpected blessings that come when you take that leap—they are worth every ounce of courage it takes.

That closet—the dark, frightening place that once held me captive—taught me something invaluable. It showed me that fear is real, but it's not insurmountable. Yes, fear tries to take root in our lives. Yes, it tries to keep us small. But when we find the courage to face it, to take even the smallest step toward healing, we find a life that is bigger, richer, and more beautiful than we could have imagined.

> *"Fear tries to convince us that we are still trapped in the darkness of our past, but the truth is, we hold the key to unlock the door and step into our freedom."*

Chapter 18

The Weight of Loyalty

I had a friend I'd always been close to—a woman with a heart that was undeniably beautiful, but like all of us, she had her struggles. We grew up together, navigated the ups and downs of our teenage years, and dreamt big dreams of who we'd become. We envisioned ourselves as Boss Ladies, building powerful, independent lives together. We promised each other that we'd be more, do more, and lift each other to new heights.

But, as the years went by, our paths began to look different. While I was ready to take the leaps, she was hesitating, her feet rooted in fear. I was stepping forward in faith, and she remained in place, moving nowhere at all. Life pulled me in another direction, and I moved away to California with my husband and children—determined to build the life I had always dreamed of.

My world started to change. I threw myself into a new rhythm, got involved in the church, and started living boldly. I became someone who learned openly, someone who made mistakes and grew from them, all out in the open. She, on the other hand, stayed hidden—guarded about her decisions, unwilling to show her true self. There was a difference between us: I embraced vulnerability, while she clung to secrecy.

One day, I received a call from her. I could hear the desperation in her voice—it was raw, and it shook me to my core. She said she needed me, and even though I lived miles away, I felt that pull to be there. It terrified me to think of her alone, at the end of her rope, so against my husband's wishes and with money we couldn't afford to spend, I bought a plane ticket and flew to her.

The plan was simple: she'd pick me up from the airport, and together we'd head to our home in Little Rock to talk, to be there for each other like we always promised we would be. But she didn't show up. I waited, and I waited some more, only to find out she wasn't in distress at all. She was with her boyfriend—her married boyfriend—and she was using my visit as a cover.

I had flown across the country, left my family behind, sacrificed our savings, and there I was stranded, alone, and betrayed. The person who said she needed me had used me, left me in the dark, and abandoned me when I needed her to simply be honest. The moment I realized what was happening, I felt my heart shatter. I had given my all, again and again, for someone who was never truly showing up for me.

The pain was deep, and the betrayal felt like a wound that would never heal. But it wasn't just about that one moment; it was the culmination of years of bending, breaking, and compromising for her. I kept giving, and she kept taking— leaving me depleted, while she moved on without a second thought.

And here is what I learned: this was more than a friendship gone wrong—this was a trauma bond. It was a relationship rooted not in genuine support, but in shared pain, a connection that had more to do with survival than it did with love.

Trauma bonding is when we feel deeply loyal to someone, not because of the love they give us, but because of the fear, the chaos, and the survival we share. It's an emotional bond that is hard to break because it's born from the parts of ourselves that are wounded, the parts that crave belonging so desperately we'll take it in any form.

For years, I believed that love meant showing up for others no matter the cost. I believed my worth was tied to how much I could give, how much I could sacrifice. And so, I gave everything—even when it left me empty. I feared what it would mean if I didn't show up for her. I feared rejection. I feared losing that connection. But in doing so, I abandoned myself.

Here's the truth: love is not supposed to leave you broken. Love is not about pouring out all you have until there's nothing left. Real love is reciprocal. It involves respect, accountability, and the courage to face hard truths without manipulating or twisting them to serve selfish needs. True love means both people are willing to grow, to heal, and to show up—even when it's uncomfortable.

Breaking Free from Trauma Bonds

I knew it was time to end this pattern. I had to let go, not because I didn't care, but because I finally understood that I had to care for myself first. Breaking that trauma bond was not easy—it was one of the hardest things I've ever done. It meant acknowledging the truth of what our relationship really was and accepting that love shouldn't hurt like this.

Here's what I learned:

1. Recognize the Signs of Trauma Bonding

Trauma bonds are deceptive because they feel like loyalty. But if you find yourself constantly feeling depleted, manipulated, or hurt, it's time to ask whether the connection is serving your well-being or just keeping you in survival mode.

2. Set Boundaries Without Guilt

Boundaries are not selfish—they are a form of self-respect. I had to learn to say no, even to people I loved. And I had to trust that my worth was not dependent on how much I gave away. Saying no isn't rejection—it's choosing to honor your needs.

3. Demand Accountability

Healthy relationships require accountability. When I realized she refused to take responsibility for her actions, I knew I had to stop making excuses. Real love requires both people to own their part and work towards doing better.

4. Trust Your Own Needs

My biggest revelation was that my needs were valid. I was worthy of love, of respect, of boundaries, without having to prove it through sacrifice. I had to learn to trust myself enough to believe that I deserved healthy love.

Stepping Into Freedom

Letting go of that trauma bond gave me freedom—freedom to see my worth without bending to make someone else feel better. It taught me that I am worthy of being loved without conditions. I am enough, not because of what I do for others, but simply because I am.

Breaking trauma bonds isn't about rejecting love—it's about redefining it. It's about recognizing that love is meant to be healing, not harmful. It's about knowing that true love is a two-way street—it is giving, yes, but it is also receiving in equal measure. It is showing up for each other, but it is also showing up for ourselves.

And the greatest lesson I learned is this: Love is not meant to break you. Love is meant to build you, heal you, and allow you to grow.

If you find yourself caught in a relationship that leaves you empty, ask yourself—are you staying out of fear, or are you staying because it helps you grow? Are you showing love, or are you just proving your worth?

The biggest blessings in my life came when I let go of the need to please, the need to sacrifice myself just to keep a connection alive. There is a whole, beautiful life waiting for us on the other side of fear—a life of freedom, joy, and real, unconditional love.

> *"Real love doesn't leave you feeling depleted—it leaves you feeling whole. When you are ready to let go of what no longer*

serves you, you open your heart to the love that truly nourishes your soul."

Chapter 19

Empowered by NO

There was a time when I believed my worth was tied to how much I could give to others, how often I said yes, how well I met everyone's expectations. And oh, how I tried to be everything to everyone—to please, to comfort, to show up for everyone who needed me, all while pretending I didn't need anything myself. I was taught that being a good person meant always saying yes, always being available, always putting others first.

In a world that often celebrates the hustle and the "yes" mentality, learning to say no was a revelation—one that forced me to look deep within myself. I realized that my constant need to say yes wasn't about kindness; it was about fear. Fear of rejection. Fear of being seen as less than. Fear of losing the acceptance and validation I so desperately craved.

The truth was, I wasn't just afraid of disappointing others—I was terrified of being rejected if I didn't perform, didn't give, didn't show up. And so, I did it all, and in the process, I became exhausted, depleted, and, most painfully, disconnected from myself.

The Meltdown

It all came to a head one day when I found myself double-booked—something I had done time and time again. I had said yes to a family event and yes to a community meeting, and suddenly, I was torn between two important parts of my life. I was overwhelmed, frantic, desperate to figure out how to be in two places at once, and I couldn't take it anymore.

I remember standing in my kitchen, tears streaming down my face, as I looked at my husband. I broke down and said, "I can't keep doing this. I just can't." My husband, in all his wisdom and love, looked at me and said something that would change my life: "You have to learn to say no. You can't be everything to everyone. You can't be a mother to our children, a wife to me, a leader in your work, and a friend to everyone without taking care of yourself first."

In that moment, it was like a light bulb turned on in my soul. I realized that my inability to say no wasn't just about overcommitment—it was about a deep-seated fear of not being enough. And the irony was, in trying to be everything for everyone, I was losing myself. I was giving so much that there was nothing left for me.

The Journey to Boundaries

So, I began a journey—a journey that started with one of the most powerful words I could speak: *no*.

At first, it was hard. Every time I said no, I felt the fear bubble up inside of me. What if they don't like me anymore? What if they think I'm selfish? What if I lose them? But I pushed through. I learned that *no* is not a rejection—it's an affirmation of self-care. It's a way of honoring my needs and trusting that the people who truly love me will respect my boundaries.

I started small. When someone invited me to an event that I wasn't up to attending, I'd take a deep breath and say, "I appreciate the invitation, but I can't make it." And you know what? The world didn't end. People didn't hate me. They still loved me. And in that process, I started to love myself a little more too.

The Power of No

I learned that saying no didn't push people away—it brought them closer. My relationships became deeper, more authentic, because I was showing up as myself, not as someone who was constantly trying to please. I realized that the people who really loved me didn't need me to be perfect. They didn't need me to always say yes. They needed me— the real me, with boundaries, with needs, with imperfections.

Saying no allowed me to create space for myself—space to breathe, space to rest, space to nurture my spirit. And as I did, I became a better mother, a better wife, a better friend. I showed up for the people I loved not because I felt obligated, but because I wanted to—because I had taken the time to fill my own cup first.

Finding Balance

Through this journey, I found something I hadn't had in a long time—balance. I was no longer juggling ten different roles, trying to keep everyone happy while I sank into exhaustion. Instead, I was living my life with intention, choosing where my energy went, and, most importantly, choosing myself first.

And let me tell you, it was liberating. Saying no was not about closing doors—it was about opening the door to a life of peace, authenticity, and deep connection. It was about learning that I am enough—not because of what I do for others, but because of who I am.

Embracing the Power of No

As I stepped into this new chapter of my life, I learned that boundaries are not walls. They are bridges. Bridges to healthier relationships. Bridges to deeper connection. Bridges to self-love. Saying no became a powerful affirmation of my worth—a declaration that my needs matter too.

When you say no, you're not rejecting others—you're honoring yourself. And when you honor yourself, you're able to show up for the people you love from a place of fullness, not emptiness.

If you are struggling to set boundaries, remember this: Saying no is an act of love for yourself, and it's through that love that you create space for deeper connections with others. You don't have to be everything for everyone to be worthy. You are enough just as you are. When you start to honor yourself, when you start to say yes to your own needs, you create a life that is rooted in authenticity, abundance, and joy.

So, say no when you need to. Say no when it's too much. Say no because you deserve to have space for yourself. And in doing so, watch your life transform. Because true love—real love—starts with the love you give yourself. And there is nothing more powerful than a woman who knows how to love herself fully.

Chapter 20

Abandonment's weight

I was married for only about a year when I found myself standing in the checkout line at Home Depot. It was supposed to be an ordinary day—just a simple errand. I was ready to make my purchase, but when I swiped my card, it declined. I tried again, but still, it declined. My heart sank, and an icy wave of panic washed over me. My first thought was not about an error, not about a bank problem. No. My first thought was that my husband had abandoned me—that he had taken the little money we had and left.

Now, you might wonder why someone would jump to such a conclusion. Why would someone imagine the worst about the person they loved? But for me, the idea of abandonment was never far from the surface. It haunted every relationship, every connection. And here I was, vulnerable, having taken a chance on marriage, still carrying the fear that one day, I'd be left behind again. As it turned out, the problem wasn't my husband—it was an expired card. But in those moments of panic, it wasn't the card that mattered; it was the echo of abandonment that spoke the loudest.

The Burden of Abandonment

The truth is, the pain of abandonment doesn't just fade—it lingers, shaping the way you think, the way you act, the way you love. It builds walls and casts shadows over even the brightest of moments. Abandonment had left its mark on me in countless ways. One of the simplest but most telling signs was my unwillingness to let anyone drop me off anywhere. Not even my husband. The fear that they wouldn't return, or that they'd come back far too late, was too strong to ignore. Every time someone said they were coming but didn't show up, that fear dug deeper into my heart, becoming more and more a part of me.

I remember vividly the time my mom must have been struggling to make ends meet, and she made the difficult decision to leave me with my father. I remember her crying, saying she didn't want to leave me, but what I remember even more was my own tears as I watched her drive away. I didn't want to stay there. It wasn't a long time, just a short while, but the memory haunted me long after. It planted a seed of doubt about my place in this world—a doubt that I carried well into adulthood.

A Lonely Night in Byhalia

There was another time when I was thirteen. My mom was living in Memphis, and my family was in Byhalia. She had given me permission to spend time with my friends, and I had felt a small sense of freedom—just a teenage girl enjoying an ordinary day. But when I returned, she was gone. She had gone back home to Memphis, and when I finally managed to reach her by phone, she told me to stay at my grandmother's house.

But my grandmother hadn't been asked, and she was upset. She told me I couldn't stay. I remember sitting on that porch that night, feeling the sting of rejection—the feeling that no one wanted me, that no one cared enough to think about where I would end up. I sat there, alone, under the darkening sky, feeling the cold weight of abandonment settle over me once more. For years, I was angry—angry at my mother, angry at my grandmother. But as I grew older, I began to understand their perspectives. I understood the struggles, the burdens, and the mistakes. But even understanding couldn't erase the pain, and the scars it left behind were real.

The Stigma of Being "Abandoned"

When I was fourteen, I made up my mind that I must have been adopted. It was the only explanation that made sense to me. I felt like I didn't belong—not with my mom's side of the family, not with my dad's. I was different, and I was alone. By then, I was also a mother myself, only fourteen and already feeling like life had written me off.

I remember going to Social Services. They handed me a folder with my name on it, and there, stamped on the front, was one word: ABANDONED. It felt like a confirmation of everything I had feared—like the world had labeled me, decided my fate, and sealed my story before I even had a chance to write it. That single word spoke of rejection, of not being wanted, of being disposable. And though I tried to push it aside, to convince myself it didn't define me, it stayed with me, feeding into every insecurity I carried.

Learning to Trust, Learning to Love

When I met my husband, I was still carrying that fear—still believing that sooner or later, he would leave. The love he offered me felt like something I couldn't trust, something that might be snatched away at any moment. I couldn't fully accept it because I was always waiting for the other shoe to drop, always preparing myself for the day he would decide I wasn't worth it and walk away. I had learned to brace for impact, to expect abandonment before it happened, as if somehow that would soften the blow.

But loving with that kind of fear isn't really love at all. It's survival. It's guarding your heart against the hurt you've already endured a thousand times over. And for a long time, that's what I did. I tried to love, but I kept my guard up, always ready to run, always prepared for the moment I would be left alone again.

But then, slowly, something began to change. It wasn't easy, and it wasn't quick. It was a process—a gradual letting go, a gentle unraveling of the walls I had built. I began to see that my husband wasn't going anywhere. He showed up every day, even when I pushed him away, even when I expected the worst of him. He was patient with my fear, and over time, I realized that the love he was offering me was real. It wasn't conditional. It wasn't something I had to earn. It was simply there, waiting for me to accept it.

The Freedom of Loving Without Fear

Learning to trust and to love without the fear of abandonment was one of the hardest things I've ever done. It required me to confront my past, to sit with the pain I had been running from, and to make peace with it. It meant understanding that my mother's choices, my father's absence, my grandmother's rejection—none of those things defined me. They were pieces of my story, but they weren't the whole story. They weren't the end.

I had to learn that the word *abandoned* on that file didn't determine my value. I had to rewrite that narrative for myself. I had to choose to believe that I was worthy of love, not because of anything I had done or anything I could prove, but simply because I was. I had to learn to trust—not just my husband, but myself. I had to trust that I was capable of being loved, that I was deserving of a love that stayed.

And as I let go of the fear, something incredible happened. I began to feel free. Free to love my husband with my whole heart, free to let him in without holding back. Free to love myself, to forgive myself for the things I had carried for so long. Free to live without the weight of expecting abandonment at every turn.

The Lesson: Choosing to Stay Open

Abandonment leaves scars, but it doesn't have to be the end of the story. It's true that the people who should have been there for me weren't always there. It's true that I was left, that I was hurt, that I was labeled. But it's also true that I have the power to choose how I move forward. I can choose to stay closed off, to guard myself against the possibility of pain. Or I can choose to stay open, to risk the hurt, because love, when it's true, is worth every risk.

Loving without fear doesn't mean that the fear disappears. It means you feel it, acknowledge it, and still choose to open your heart. It means you decide that your past doesn't get to dictate your future. It means choosing to believe that you are enough, just as you are, and that you deserve a love that stays.

Abandonment may be a part of my story, but it is not the whole story. The real story is about resilience. It's about choosing to trust, even when trust feels impossible. It's about loving with abandon, even when love has hurt you before. It's about knowing that you are worthy—not because of anything you've done, but simply because you exist.

Today, I stand in that truth. I am not abandoned. I am not unwanted. I am loved, deeply and completely, and I choose to love in return. Not with fear, not with hesitation, but with an open heart. And that, I have found, is where the real healing begins.

> *"The wound is where the light enters you."*
>
> —Rumi

Chapter 21

Owning My Space

Ah, imposter syndrome—what a peculiar companion it can be. It doesn't show up when you're just getting started, struggling to find your way. No, it waits until you're standing at the very doorstep of the life you've built, the success you've earned. Just when you've arrived at that long-awaited destination, it creeps in to whisper, "You don't belong here."

I remember that feeling so vividly, standing at what I thought would be the pinnacle—the place I had dreamed of, worked for, sacrificed for. I had given everything to become someone I could be proud of, someone my children could look up to. The sleepless nights, the sacrifices, the countless times I faced my fears and pushed through—I had done it all. I was relentless. I built my business, I created financial security, I worked on my marriage, I healed. I wasn't just surviving, I was thriving.

But then, upon arrival, I felt... like a fraud. It was as if all the work I had done, all the steps I had taken, suddenly didn't matter. Somewhere deep inside, there was this nagging voice saying, any minute now, they'll find out. Any minute now, they'll see that you don't belong.

Those voices from my past echoed louder and louder: reminding me of all the instability, the pain, the hardships that marked my earlier years. They whispered, Who do you think you are to be here? People like you don't deserve this kind of life. The voices of doubt tried to take me down, to strip me of the pride and joy I had worked so hard for.

That's the thing about imposter syndrome—it convinces you that you're here by accident, that you're standing in a space that doesn't truly belong to you. It tries to convince you that your achievements were mere luck, that your work somehow doesn't count, that the success others see is just an illusion.

But I had to fight those voices. Every single day, I had to remind myself: I belong here. I am here because I worked for it, because I faced my challenges, because I did not let fear have the last word. I belong here because I chose courage over comfort, because I embraced healing, because I made a decision to thrive, not just survive.

You see, imposter syndrome is a liar. It tells us we need to be perfect, flawless, untouched by struggle, in order to deserve the life we've built. But the truth is, it's the struggle, it's the scars, it's the journey through pain and doubt that make our achievements real. I had to learn to embrace every part of my story—to own the instability, the mistakes, the challenges, and recognize that they were all stepping stones. They didn't disqualify me; they prepared me for this very moment.

> *"I had to remind myself often: The place where you are standing, the space that you've worked so hard to step into, is not a mistake—it is yours by right, because you did the work, you faced the challenges, and you grew beyond what anyone expected."*

111

I had to redefine what worthiness looked like. I had to redefine success. I began to see that perfection wasn't the goal—realness was. I could stand tall, not because I was without flaw, but because I had faced my fears, moved beyond my past, and dared to dream bigger. I could be proud of where I was, not despite my journey, but because of it.

And here's what I want you to know: If you're battling imposter syndrome, you are not alone. The very fact that you're here, standing on the threshold of your dreams, means you've already defied the odds. You've pushed beyond what seemed possible, you've risen above your circumstances, and you have earned your place. You belong here.

Here are the truths I had to hold onto as I fought the voices of doubt:

- ↔ You did the work. All those sacrifices, all those moments of courage when you chose to show up even when it was hard—those weren't accidents. They were real, and they were yours. You're not an imposter; you're the author of your journey.

- ↔ Your past does not disqualify you. Where you've come from adds richness to where you are now. It's the very proof of your strength. Your past is part of your story, but it doesn't determine your future. You belong here, not despite your past, but because you've risen above it.

- ↔ Perfection is not the requirement. You do not need to be flawless to be deserving. Your worth isn't based on perfection—it's rooted in your persistence, your courage, and your resilience. Acknowledge your accomplishments, every one of them, and know that they are well-earned.

↦ There is room for you. You are not taking anyone else's space by thriving. The life you've built is yours because you made it so. There is room enough in this world for everyone to shine, including you. Take your seat at the table. Own it.

↦ Imposter syndrome may still come knocking, trying to make you believe that you're not enough. But let it be a reminder that you are growing, that you're stepping into the life that you were meant to have. You belong here. And the best way to quiet those voices of doubt is to keep moving, keep growing, and keep embracing every part of who you are.

↦ You are not an imposter. You are not a mistake. You are worthy of every blessing that has come your way, because you worked for it, because you chose healing, because you dared to dream, and because you believed.

> *"Step fully into the space you've earned, the life you've created. You belong here. The best is yet to come."*

Chapter 22

Next Chapter

Choosing healing after trauma is not a simple, linear process. Healing, my friends, is not a straight line where each day is brighter, each step lighter. It doesn't work that way. Healing is messy. It is unpredictable. It is often uncomfortable. Some days you feel like you can conquer the world, and other days it feels as if the weight of your past is pulling you under again. But with each step, no matter how small, I feel a renewed sense of hope—a belief that, yes, I can overcome.

Healing asks us to be brave, to confront those parts of ourselves that hurt the most. It requires us to look into the mirror of our pain and say, "I am here. I am not running anymore." And let me tell you, it is not easy. But it is also beautiful. Healing is about embracing who you are, with all the flaws, all the scars, and allowing yourself to be imperfect. It's about giving yourself permission to stumble and still rise again.

To you, dear reader, I want you to understand this: healing is not about perfection. It is not about erasing the past or pretending it didn't happen. Healing is about acceptance— accepting the things you cannot change, accepting yourself as you are now, and opening your heart to the love and support you deserve. There is no right or wrong way to heal. Each of us has our own path, our own journey. Every single step, no matter how small, is a step forward.

There will be moments when you feel as though the pain is insurmountable, moments when you wonder if it's worth it. There will be days when giving up seems easier. But let me tell you—those moments are when you need to keep going. Those moments are when you need to dig deep and remember why you started this journey in the first place. The journey of healing is not easy, but it is worth every moment of effort. Healing is about finding the strength to keep moving forward, even when the path ahead is uncertain, and trusting that, with time, the pain will lessen, and the wounds will begin to heal.

I am learning, slowly, to embrace this journey. I am learning to appreciate the small victories along the way. To celebrate those tiny moments of progress, even when they seem insignificant. When I find myself responding to a situation with calm instead of fear, or when I allow myself to truly feel joy without the shadow of the past hanging over me, I know I am healing. I am learning that healing doesn't mean I will never feel pain again. No, it means that I am no longer defined by that pain. It means I am learning to move through it rather than allowing it to dictate my every move.

And as I reflect on my own healing process, I feel an overwhelming sense of gratitude. There was a time when I believed my past was a burden I would carry forever—a time when the weight of my pain felt too heavy to bear. But here I am, standing in the light of a new day. I am not just a survivor; I am a woman who has faced the depths of pain and emerged with a new sense of purpose, with love, with self-acceptance. I am stronger for it. I am grateful for it.

And to you, I want to say this: You are not alone in your healing journey. There are others who have walked this path before you, who have struggled, who have fallen, and who have risen again. Healing takes time. It requires patience, but you are stronger than you know. The very fact that you are here, reading these words, means that you have already taken a step toward something better. It means you have the strength, the resilience, and the courage to change your story.

Choosing to heal is not just about transforming your own life—it's about paving the way for those who come after you. I am healing not only for myself but also for my kids. I want them to grow up in a world filled with love, with stability, with resilience. I want them to see what it means to be strong, to face your fears, and to choose yourself every single day. Together, we are on this journey of healing—a journey that honors where we've come from while embracing all that lies ahead.

I want you to remember this: healing is not about erasing the past. It's about learning to carry it in a way that no longer weighs you down. It's about understanding that the pain you've experienced does not define you. You are more than the hurt. You are more than the trauma. You are deserving of love, of joy, of peace.

It's okay to take your time. It's okay to feel lost sometimes. But know that every step you take is bringing you closer to a version of yourself that is more aligned, more at peace, more whole. Healing is about writing a new chapter in your story—a chapter that is filled with hope, with courage, and with love. You are not broken. You are in the process of becoming, of growing. You are worthy of the life you desire, and you are capable of achieving it.

So, as you move forward, remember: healing is not about never feeling pain again. It's about learning how to navigate that pain, how to hold it without letting it define you. It's about learning to live fully, to love deeply, and to embrace the beauty of each new day.

A new chapter begins today. One where you choose yourself, where you honor your journey, where you take each step with the courage to face whatever comes next. You have the strength to overcome, the resilience to rise, and the capacity to heal. This is your journey, your new beginning, and it is filled with possibilities beyond measure.

Keep moving forward. The best, my friend, is yet to come.

> *"Healing isn't about erasing the past; it's about learning to carry it with grace. It's about understanding that your pain is part of your story, but it doesn't define your future."*

Chapter 23

Embracing Growth

Change and growth, they rarely unfold the way we expect them to. I used to think growth was a straightforward journey—one where you move steadily forward, where each step leads you to a brighter, clearer day. But what I've learned is that real growth doesn't follow a straight line. It doesn't come easily wrapped up in a neat bow.

No, growth is full of detours, unexpected roadblocks, and moments that make you question whether you're even on the right path.

If life had followed the plan, I once had for it, I would have found peace much sooner. But, oh, how much I would have missed! Because peace isn't a destination; it's what you find in the journey—in the mess, in the stumbling, in the picking yourself back up again. It's in the uncomfortable spaces, in the moments that challenge everything you thought you knew. It's when you fall down and decide, "This isn't how my story ends."

When I began my healing journey, I had this image in my mind that each day would be a little easier, that I'd feel just a bit lighter every morning. But healing doesn't work that way. It's not this beautiful, upward climb. It's more like a dance—sometimes you move forward, and other times you step back, sometimes you spin in circles and lose your balance. But each step, each movement, is a part of your journey, and every step matters, even the backward ones.

I used to think setbacks meant I wasn't doing something right, that maybe I just wasn't capable of real change. But I now see that setbacks aren't failures—they are invitations. They invite us to dig deeper, to understand the parts of ourselves that still need healing. They remind us that growth isn't about erasing our past; it's about understanding it more deeply, about finding new ways to move forward with it instead of in spite of it.

Setbacks and Breakthroughs

I remember a time when I thought I had finally turned a corner in my healing. I had done the work—therapy, journaling, praying, and taking care of myself. For a moment, I felt a sense of freedom from the weight of my past. But freedom, I found, can be fleeting. Life has a way of testing what you've learned, of asking you, "Are you really ready for the next level?"

Not long after that breakthrough, I was faced with a painful breakup—a relationship I had poured my heart into was suddenly unraveling. And with it, all those old wounds of rejection and abandonment came rushing back, crashing over me like a tidal wave. I felt like I was right back where I started, drowning in the same fears, the same doubts. I remember sitting alone, crying out, "Why am I back here?

Why does this hurt so much?" In that moment, it felt like I had failed.

But what I know now is that healing is about peeling back layers. Just when you think you've healed, life will give you another layer to work through—not to punish you, but to help you go deeper. Healing isn't about never feeling pain again; it's about learning to carry it differently each time it resurfaces.

Growth in the Stuckness

There were other times, times when I felt like I was making no progress at all. Times when I was trying to build my business and nothing seemed to move. I felt stagnant, like all my efforts were for nothing. My inner critic would whisper, "Maybe you're not cut out for this. Maybe this dream is too big for you." And let me tell you, those whispers are loud when you're already questioning yourself. I felt like I was failing not just in my work, but in my life—in my role as a mother, a leader, a partner.

But here's the truth I discovered: growth doesn't always look like movement. Sometimes, growth looks like stillness. Sometimes, it looks like being stuck. Being stuck isn't the absence of growth; it's often the most powerful place for transformation. In the stillness, in the waiting, in the places where it feels like nothing is happening—that's where we are being molded and prepared for what's to come.

I came to understand that those seasons of feeling stuck were not punishments—they were times of preparation. Times when I needed to pause, to learn, to grow internally in ways that weren't immediately visible. Because the truth is, the dreams we have—the big, audacious dreams—they require a version of us that we're still becoming. And the becoming happens in the quiet, in the uncomfortable waiting.

The Messy Middle

Ah, the messy middle. The part of the journey that is so often overlooked but is where the real magic happens. It's that in-between space—between who you were and who you are becoming. It's messy because you're letting go of old patterns while trying to embrace new ones. It's chaotic because you're shedding parts of yourself that no longer serve you, while still figuring out who you want to be.

One of the hardest things I ever did was step into my role as a leader—not just in my work, but in my life. For so long, I stayed small. I avoided attention, avoided conflict, avoided anything that might put me in the spotlight. So, when I started stepping into leadership, it was terrifying. I doubted myself constantly, questioned if I was worthy of guiding others when I was still figuring things out for myself.

But here's what I learned in that messy middle: you don't need to be perfect to lead. You don't need to have all the answers to take a step forward. Growth happens in the moments when you choose to show up, even when it's uncomfortable. When you choose to lead, not because you have it all figured out, but because you believe in the possibility of what could be.

Lessons Learned on Growth and Change

1. *Let Go of the Timeline:* Growth doesn't happen on your schedule. It doesn't fit neatly into your plans. Let go of the idea that you should be further along by now. Trust that you are exactly where you need to be, right here, right now.

2. *Embrace the Setbacks:* Setbacks aren't failures; they're opportunities for deeper healing. Each setback is an invitation to learn, to grow, and to understand yourself more fully.

3. *Trust the Process:* Growth requires trust—trust in yourself, trust in the journey, and trust in the timing. Even when you can't see the progress, trust that it's happening. Growth is often invisible before it becomes undeniable.

4. *Find Peace in the Messy Middle:* Embrace the uncomfortable space between who you were and who you're becoming. Let yourself be in the transition, knowing that the mess is where you are being refined.

5. *Celebrate Small Wins:* Growth doesn't always come in big, transformative moments. Sometimes, it's in the quiet victories—the days you choose to get up, to try again, to love yourself a little more. Celebrate those moments.

Becoming Who You're Meant to Be

The journey of growth and change isn't about becoming someone new. It's about uncovering the truest version of yourself—the version that was always there, underneath the fear, the doubt, and the pain. Growth is messy, yes. It's uncomfortable. But it's also where the magic happens, where you discover who you truly are, where the real transformation begins.

Every setback, every time you feel stuck, every time you question whether you're moving in the right direction—it's all a part of the process. Every moment, no matter how difficult, is leading you closer to the person you are meant to be.

Embrace the journey. Trust that even when you can't see the way forward, growth is happening. It's happening in the stillness, in the waiting, in the mess. You are growing. You are becoming. And the best is yet to come.

> *"Growth isn't a straight line—it's a journey through detours, setbacks, and moments of stillness. True transformation happens not in the absence of struggle, but in the messy, uncomfortable spaces where we choose to keep moving forward despite it all."*

Closing Thoughts

Healing is a journey, not a destination. This is just a beginning, an invitation to step forward, one day at a time. It's not about getting it perfect; it's about showing up, about being willing to do the work, even on the days when it's hard.

Eighteen years have passed since I took that leap of faith, and today, my life is more than I could have imagined. My husband and I have faced trials, experienced triumphs, and grown together in ways I never thought possible. We're raising six beautiful children, building a business, and living a life of purpose—a life that once felt like a distant dream. And all of it began with a willingness to say yes to myself, to say yes to the work, to say yes to healing.

To anyone who feels stuck, who feels like they're carrying too much to move forward, I want you to remember this: "The journey to healing doesn't require perfection—it only requires courage. Courage to take that first step, courage to face what's in the mirror, and courage to keep moving forward, no matter how messy it gets."

There is beauty on the other side of your fears. There is joy beyond the pain. There is a future waiting for you that is full of possibility. Keep showing up for yourself. Keep taking each small step. The best is yet to come.